£5.95

THE ORGANIC HANDBO

Healthy Fruit and Vegetables

How to avoid diseases, disorders and deficiencies

Pauline Pears and Bob Sherman

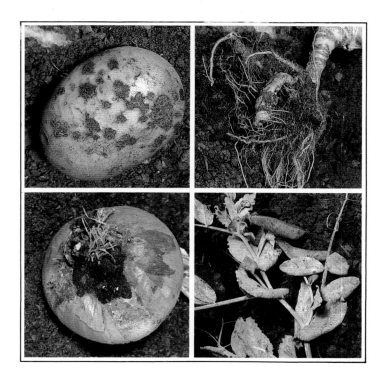

Henry Doubleday Research Association/Search Press

First published in Great Britain 1991
Search Press Ltd.,
Wellwood, North Farm Road,
Tunbridge Wells, Kent TN2 3DR

in association with

The Henry Doubleday Research Association,
National Centre for Organic Gardening,
Ryton-on-Dunsmore,
Coventry CV8 3LG

Illustrations by Polly Pinder
Photographs by Charlotte de la Bedoyère

The publishers would like to thank the National Institute of
Agricultural Botany (N.I.A.B.) for their help in providing some
of the diseases for photographic purposes.

ISBN 0 85532 689 1

Conversion Chart

From centimetres to inches		From grammes to ounces	
1 cm	= ½ in	7 g =	¼ oz
2.5 cm	= 1 in	14 g =	½ oz
5 cm	= 2 in	28 g =	1 oz
10 cm	= 4 in	110 g =	4 oz
50 cm	= 20 in	450 g =	16 oz (1 lb)
100 cm (1 m)	= 40 in	From litres to pints	
1 sq m	= 1.2 sq yds	1 l = 1.75 pt	

Exact conversions from imperial to metric
measures are not possible, so the metric
measures have been rounded up.

Phototypeset by Scribe Design.
Printed in Spain by Elkar S. Coop.

Introduction

The simplest and most effective way of dealing with diseases, disorders and deficiencies in a garden — whether it is run organically or otherwise — is to create an environment in which they are unlikely to occur in the first place.

There are many ways of making your garden a healthy place for fruit and vegetables to grow, and we have devoted the first part of the book to showing how this can be achieved. The second part of the book moves on to the diseases, disorders and deficiencies that may affect your crops. We have, inevitably, had to limit the number included, but have aimed to select the most common. We start with the more widespread problems that may affect many different types of plant. Diseases, disorders and deficiencies that affect specific fruits and vegetables are listed in the chart that follows. In every case, symptoms are described and details given of what steps to take to avoid the problem, or what to do if your plants are already affected. Information is also given on the lifestyle and habits of the disease-causing organisms; knowing more can make dealing with a problem easier and can help avert panic!

The great difficulty in a book on this subject is identification. This is a problem not only for the gardener, but often for the expert as well. Wherever possible, illustrations have been included to help. These, although accurate, can be misleading and should not be used *on their own* to identify a problem. You will soon find out for yourself that similar symptoms can have several different causes.

Finally, remember that few diseases are catastrophic, and in most cases your crop can be saved. Disorders are often caused by weather conditions beyond your control — the bane of every gardener. Deficiencies, although aggravating at the time, can usually be put right for future seasons.

A possible garden plan   r. = rotation

How to grow healthy plants

Soil

No plant will thrive on a poor diet and in an adverse environment. It only has the choice that you make for it, so it is vital that its food source, the soil, is well managed. Acidity, availability of nutrients and structure all affect the growth of your plants. Inattention to these might hinder growth or induce strange symptoms caused by mineral deficiencies and will certainly make your plants more likely to succumb to disease.

Know your soil
Getting to know your soil starts by picking up a damp handful and feeling it.

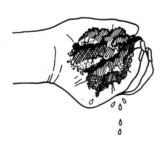

If it sticks together readily when squeezed, then you have a heavy soil that probably drains badly and becomes hard and solid when dry.

If it feels gritty and is not sticky, then you have a light soil which lacks body and will dry out quickly. Both are greatly improved by the use of compost, manure, leaf mould and other sources of organic matter.

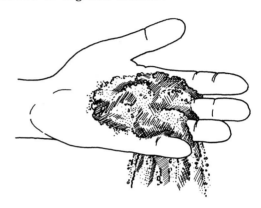

Soil analysis
Simple observation of the plants, or even weeds, growing in your garden will give some indication of the nutritional content of your soil. Spindly growth and pale leaves may indicate a shortage of nitrogen. A detailed and accurate portrait can be obtained from a professional soil analysis, preferably from a laboratory offering a fully organic service. The soil report will show not only the level of important nutrients but also the degree of acidity (pH). More details on this subject, and information about how to correct any deficiencies and build a healthy soil, can be found in the companion volumes in this series, *Soil Care and Management* by Jo Readman, and *How to make your Garden Fertile* by Pauline Pears.

Problems with water

Too much water
Poor drainage can either be natural or caused by man's use of the land. It is easily spotted after heavy rain; puddles form or an area remains boggy long after surrounding soil has drained.

Various causes of poor drainage

● *Cause* – poor soil structure. Possible on any soil but more likely on heavy clay or silt soils. Visible as severe cracking even in dry weather.

● *Remedy* – improve soil structure. Incorporate plenty of organic matter. Use mulches. Apply ground limestone or dolomite to acid clay. On alkaline clay use gypsum or seaweed meal. Coarse grit is also useful for heavy soils.

● *Cause* – compaction. Usually a result of walking on cultivated areas. Also likely after builders' traffic, especially on recently completed housing sites.

● *Remedy* – eliminate need to walk on soil by using a 'bed' system of growing. Cure compaction by digging. Double digging may be necessary in severe cases.

● *Cause* – sub-surface pan or impermeable layer. High levels of some minerals, such as iron and aluminium, can cause very hard solidified layers by natural process. These layers can be very deep. A similar effect occurs if a rotovator is used regularly as the only means of turning the soil. The soil becomes polished and less permeable at the level reached by the tines.

● *Remedy* – cure a relatively shallow pan by digging. Deeper problems can only be cured by laying drainage pipes or using agricultural subsoiling machinery.

● *Cause* – high water table. A natural phenomenon. It is hard to grow healthy fruit and vegetables on such sites.

● *Remedy* – artificial drainage. A major undertaking.

Too little water

Plants need water just to survive. There are also a number of disorders caused by heavy rain following a very dry spell: roots can split, tomato skins crack and potatoes become deformed.

Parched soils are as unwelcome as saturated bogs. Good drainage does not preclude the ability of a soil to hold water. The ideal conditions for growth include a constant evenly moist soil around the root area with no extremes of dry and wet. Sandy soils drain well so they rarely become waterlogged but can easily dry out in prolonged hot spells. Clay soils, on the other hand, can retain water which, because of the soil's structure, is unavailable to the plant.

Ways to improve water supply to plants

● *Add organic matter.* This adds spongy bulk to the soil which soaks up water but allows roots to penetrate and make use of it. Compost, manure, leaf mould and green manures are all suitable. (See Organic Handbook 1, *How to make your Garden Fertile* by Pauline Pears.)

Compost

● *Use mulches.* Water percolates downwards but also evaporates upwards. A thick layer of organic matter laid over the surface prevents evaporation and saves much water. Suitable materials include hay, straw, manure, compost, leaf mould, grass mowings and shredded prunings. Mulches of polythene or woven polypropylene are also useful but not biodegradable and, in the case of polythene, do not allow rainfall to penetrate.

Artichoke with mulch of straw

Celeriac with mulch of hay

Fencing windbreak

● *Windbreaks.* Wind dehydrates plants at least as fast as sunshine. Windbreaks erected around vegetables and fruit can be limited to a single crop (e.g. courgettes) or all-embracing. They can be in the form of a hedge or specially designed artificial materials. (For further information on windbreaks see page 10.)

Plant foods

Deficiencies

A soil analysis will show the level of important minerals available to your crops. If these are low, then the deficiency can be corrected with the relevant organic fertiliser or, in some cases, an increase in organic matter. If organic matter levels are low, then organic fertilisers will be of little use on their own as the soil micro-organisms necessary for their breakdown will be weak. Poor nutrition occasionally shows itself in a garden but the symptoms and causes can be difficult to diagnose. Poor structure, flooding, dry soil and cold weather can all induce deficiencies. The chart on pages 36–59 shows some typical symptoms, with other possible causes, which make plants take on a similar appearance or which might cause a temporary food shortage. If the latter is the case, then a cure other than fertiliser will be the answer. In any case diagnosis is not easy. For this reason we have concentrated on the more common deficiencies (see pages 31–35).

Striking a balance

Weakly growing plants readily succumb to disease. The same is true of excessively lush growth, e.g. gooseberries are prone to powdery mildew if an excess of nitrogen in the soil spurs on rapid young growth.

Balanced food supplies are important, especially between the main plant foods, nitrogen, potash and phosphate. Excess of some minerals can, curiously, cause similar effects to those of a deficiency. This is less common in organically managed plots. Here, minerals are released by the breakdown of organic matter at a speed relative to a plant's growing needs. But even under an organic regime, it is possible to overfeed plants. If your soil is well fed with manure and compost, then deficiencies of major minerals and trace elements are unlikely. Your plants will be your best guide. If they are growing well, then there is no need to scatter handfuls of fertiliser around them.

Plants and places

Reducing the likelihood of disease begins with the soil and continues with the plants. There are many considerations and decisions that you can make to reduce problems in a plant's life cycle. Some of the most important occur at the very start.

Seeds

Every seed has a maximum shelf-life beyond which it will not germinate. The list below shows some examples of the life expectancy of seeds kept under average conditions, since most gardeners do not manage 'optimum conditions'. Seedlings from old seed will be less vigorous and less likely to grow into healthy plants.

Average life expectancy			
4 YEARS	3 YEARS	2 YEARS	1 YEAR
Beetroot	Broccoli	Broad beans	
Chard	Brussels sprouts	Carrot	Parsnip
Courgette	Cabbage	Leek	
Cucumber	Cauliflower	Onion	
Marrow	Lettuce	Parsley	
Pumpkin	Peas	Runner beans	
Radish	Swede	French beans	
Tomato	Turnip	Spinach	

If you are in doubt about some of your seeds, then try a simple germination test. Place 20 or more seeds on some wet tissue and keep them warm and moist. If the seeds are good, then they will produce a tiny root after a few days. Wait about seven to ten days and make a rough count of how many seeds have germinated. This will tell you what success you are likely to have with the rest of the packet.

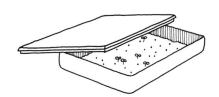

Seed storage

Do not store seeds on a greenhouse bench, in a damp shed or on a warm kitchen shelf. Ideal conditions for seed storage are a cool, dry, *constant* atmosphere. Airtight preserving jars make excellent containers if kept in a cool room. Even better, place a sachet of silica crystals in each jar to absorb moisture. Note the date of purchase of the seeds or avoid throwing away the packer's date mark on the packet (easily torn off in exuberant springtime mood).

Resistant varieties

Much current research is aimed at finding varieties of fruit and vegetables that are less susceptible to specific diseases. In some cases varieties show almost total immunity. Look out for resistant varieties in seed and plant catalogues.

Disease-free planting material

The best strawberries, fruit bushes and trees to buy are those raised from virus-free stock plants. Potato seed tubers are also possible carriers of debilitating viruses and diseases, but good suppliers will offer a virus-free guarantee. In some countries this is backed by a government certification scheme. It is generally advisable to buy new seed potatoes or strawberry runners rather than save your own.

Nurseries and garden centres sell thousands of plants. Not all will be of the best quality. Choose yours with care. Look for even growth, good shape and good roots. Avoid plants showing signs of breakage and those that are pot bound.

The ideal site

Choose the best site in your garden before wasting time, money and energy on cultivating and planting. Look for a good aspect (according to local climate), shelter (see page 10), shading, access for wheelbarrows and preferably a site with no drainage problems. For most of us the choice is limited. If this is so, then match plants to the site.

On cold sites avoid early-flowering or late-maturing fruit varieties and crops that need a long warm season, such as sweet corn or tomatoes. Keep the sunniest spot for most vegetables, strawberries, raspberries, blackcurrants, hybrid berries, apples, pears, plums and cherries. Redcurrants, gooseberries and blackberries will tolerate light shade, as will some vegetables, such as Jerusalem artichokes, fennel, rocket, spinach beet and chicories.

Weather

If the weather is fine and settled, then it is easy to forget how violent it can be! Wind and frost cause physical damage to your garden plants, providing entry points for disease spores.

Wind

High winds break branches and even tear plants out of the soil. Wind also significantly reduces the air temperature which greatly influences cropping potential and pollination of fruit.

Problems with wind can be reduced by erecting some form of windbreak

● *Windbreak netting.* Fixed to upright posts with bracing struts at corners. There are several different materials available with life expectancy varying from three to ten years. Early in the year, short-term windbreaks can be erected on canes round susceptible tender crops, such as beans, courgettes and tomatoes.

● *Fencing.* Much less permeable than windbreak netting but should last longer if good quality. Often of very solid construction which causes wind turbulence in the lee, sucking plants towards the fence. Cure by stripping off one-third of laths on alternate panels.

● *Hedges and shelter-belts.* Long-lasting, permanent and attractive. Take time to establish. Encourage wildlife. Native trees and shrubs are tougher and better for wildlife habitats. Shelter-belts are composed of shrubs and trees in a broad planting, with a line of trees on the outside and shrubs on the protected side. Plant closely (trees at 2m, shrubs at 1m) and thin after three or four years. Avoid surface-rooting plants such as privet (*Ligustrum ovalifolium*), Lawson cypress (*Chamaecyparis lawsoniana*) and Leyland cypress (× *Cupressocyparis leylandii*), which will compete with crops for water and nutrients.

Frost

Late frosts in spring and early frosts in autumn can ruin crops. Damage can be quite sudden and severe and easily mistaken for a disease.

All frost damage is a potential site for fungus entry. For example, plum blossom when bitten by frost allows brown rot fungus to enter the plant which in turn causes blossom wilt and wither tip. Early shoots of potatoes can be nipped off and young tender seedlings killed or damaged beyond recovery.

Frost damage on potato. Despite this the plot went on to produce a good crop.

Reduce the risk of frost damage

● Do not sow or plant out too early. Later sowings will rapidly catch up as soil warms.

● Cover crops with cloches or 'fleece' type crop covers to create a microclimate that keeps out one or two degrees of frost. Similar materials can be used to cover blossoming plums, cherries and pears at night when frost threatens.

● Do not cover the soil with organic mulches too early in the season. The soil acts as a 'storage heater' taking in warmth by day and releasing it at night, so keeping a certain amount of frost at bay. A mulched soil will not have this effect.

● Strawing down. At the end of the season, marrows, pumpkins, swedes, beetroot, celeriac and carrots can be protected by a layer of straw until the weather becomes very cold.

Harvesting

● If frost is forecast, then harvest tender crops in time.

● If your site is in a frost pocket or subject to unpredictable weather, then choose hardy varieties of fruit and frost-tolerant vegetables.

Good gardening

Organic gardeners do not rely on sprays to get them out of trouble. Therefore, good gardening practice is essential.

Crop rotation

The principle of crop rotation is never to follow one crop with another from the same family. Moving crops around the plots prevents the rapid build-up of soil-borne diseases. Some of these diseases, such as club root of brassicas or white rot of onions, are very hard to eradicate.

The same principle applies to fruit. After three years a strawberry crop will be less productive and more prone to virus and disease. It should be grubbed out and the land used for another type of crop. The replacement crop should be planted in a new site. After three or four years the original site should be fit for replanting. If you are clearing an old raspberry bed or renewing fruit trees or bushes, then try to find a new clean site for the replacements as far away as possible from the old one.

In the vegetable garden, plan your cropping so that you can group together (a) those plants that are prone to the same pests and diseases (b) those plants that like the same soil conditions. The longer your rotation the better. In practice, this usually means three or four years in the average garden.

Groups of crops in the same family:

- Potatoes and tomatoes.
- Onions, garlic, leeks and shallots.
- Cabbages, Brussels sprouts, cauliflowers, kale, broccoli, swedes, turnips, kohlrabies and radishes.
- Carrots, parsnips, celery, parsley and celeriac.
- Peas and beans of all sorts, winter tares.
- Courgettes, pumpkins and cucumbers.
- Lettuce, endive, chicory, salsify and scorzonera.

A circular plot for a very small garden

Effective planting

Effective planting begins with the careful preparation of your site. Dig the site, incorporating organic matter and organic fertilisers as indicated by your soil analysis and observation (see page 4). Do not dig individual planting holes for fruit trees in an otherwise uncultivated soil, especially if it is heavy. They will act as sumps for all the surplus water nearby. This is not normally a problem on light, well-drained soil.

Correct drainage

For information on correcting drainage problems see page 5.

Correct depth

Plant out seedlings without burying them too deeply. Some, however, such as tomatoes, can be planted deeply to advantage as they make extra roots along the buried stem. Others will become subject to the fungal disease damping off, normally a problem associated with seedbeds and greenhouse sowings rather than transplants.

Plant blackcurrants a few centimetres deeper than previously. All other fruit should be planted at the original depth, usually visible as a soil mark on the stem. This avoids rotting and prevents grafted trees from rooting above the graft. Do not bury strawberry crowns.

Firm soil around trees and bushes and stake them. Knock in the stake before planting to avoid breaking roots.

Timing

Do not plant out tender or less hardy seedlings if frosts are still likely, unless you can protect them with cloches. Seeds sown into cold soil germinate and grow slowly. This makes them more prone to disease.

The ideal time for planting out trees and bushes is at leaf fall or just after. At this time there is a natural surge of root growth and plants are likely to establish themselves better. If this is not possible, then plant out at some time during the dormant season. Plants grown in containers (as opposed to those lifted from the soil and containerised just prior to selling) can be planted out at any time.

However, any planting outside the dormant season will need copious watering.

Strawberries are best planted out at the end of the summer or potted up at this time for planting out in late autumn.

Correct conditions

Avoid planting into very dry or waterlogged soil. If heavy rain is forecast and ground conditions are perfect but you are not ready to plant out, then cover the soil with a polythene sheet.

Correct spacing

Very close plantings can create the still conditions that favour fungal attack. Onions can be very closely spaced but may then succumb to mildew. Close spacing of onions may also allow white rot to spread rapidly along the row because roots will be touching below the soil. Multi-sown clumps of onions, spaced 25–30 cm apart, reduce the risk of losing a whole crop – individually affected clumps can quickly be removed. On the other hand, closely spaced parsnips make smaller roots which are less likely to develop canker.

Follow instructions on seed packets or consult your local nursery. Advice on vegetable spacing varies greatly. Experience will tell you what is best in your garden. Correct spacing of plants is particularly important in fruit growing as they will have to live in the space allotted to them for many years.

Pruning

Good pruning at the right time helps rapid healing and, therefore, there is less chance of

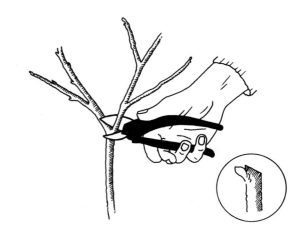

infection. Prune at an angle close to a bud without cutting too deeply behind the bud (as illustrated). Do not leave snags or ragged cuts. Keep secateurs clean and sharp.

Prune plums and cherries between June and September when risk of infection by bacterial canker and silver leaf is lower.

Remember that good air circulation within the branch canopy and between plants reduces chances of disease.

Garden hygiene

A little untidiness in the garden is good for wildlife but not ideal in the vegetable or fruit plots. By clearing away brown brassica leaves as the plants develop and in winter, you may remove spores of downy mildew, leaf spot and other fungi.

If you are pruning out diseased tissue on fruit, then remove the material to the dustbin or bonfire rather than dropping it on the ground.

Be careful what you put on the compost heap. A hot heap will kill many disease organisms but not all. If in doubt, then keep it out.

Breaking the cycle

Rows of overgrown, flowering Brussels sprouts in the late spring are not an unfamiliar sight. Clearing these and other redundant crops away to the compost heap will break the cycle of disease and pest attack because there will be no host plants left to colonise. Similarly, clear away old diseased fruit before planting new stock.

Overfeeding

Plants that are growing well do not need feeding. Too much encouragement will produce soft lush growth which is prone to disease.

Watering

Correct watering is important although there is plenty of margin for error. Too much water causes waterlogging, leading to damping off and root rots; too little leads to drought stress and possible collapse of plants. Powdery mildew is most common where plant roots are in dry soil; downy mildew and botrytis are most common in wet conditions.

Some hints and tips for watering

● Mulched soil and soil well fed on organic matter hold more water.

● A dry surface does not always mean a dry soil. Check with your finger or trowel before applying large amounts of water.

● Seedlings have few roots, all of them only just below the surface. These need regular watering in dry weather.

● Water seed drills thoroughly before, rather than after, sowing.

● A very dry soil needs more than a casual sprinkling of water on the surface; 10 litres per sq m will be needed to wet it thoroughly.

● Deep-rooting crops, such as parsnips, will find water deep in the soil once they are growing well. Wetting the surface, if the soil is dry, will discourage the crop from deep rooting.

● Raspberries have very shallow roots. Mulch them well once the soil has been warmed in spring.

● Beans and peas need little water when producing leaves. Lack of water at flowering and fruiting, however, causes poor cropping.

● Fruit trees need water during fruiting. Shortage of water causes silvering of leaves (false silver leaf) and bitter pit in apples.

● Use seep-hoses or driplines where possible so that water is applied to soil close to plants rather than wasted on paths and leaves. Bright sunshine can scorch wet leaves.

Picking off and pruning out

Inspect crops regularly. Spotting early signs of disease allows you to pick off or prune out

damage before it spreads. Dig up sick plants – they seldom recover.

Use the right product for the job

Improvisation has always been part of the enjoyment of gardening but it is advisable not to experiment with plant health. Tractor grease, for example, is not a suitable alternative for tree grease for fruit trees and may cause canker to develop.

Know your problem

Do not jump to conclusions. Before deciding on a course of action, check a plant very carefully for all the symptoms. Bear in mind that different diseases and deficiencies can often look alike, and damage caused by pests can also be similar. For example, the picture below shows damage to a redcurrant leaf that might easily be mistaken for a terrible disease. Actually, it is caused by a pest, the currant blister aphid (see our companion volume in this series, *How to control Fruit & Vegetable Pests*).

Damage caused by currant blister aphid

The following pages will help you to identify the most common crop diseases, disorders and deficiencies (but hopefully you will grow an abundance of healthy fruit and vegetables and not need to consult them too often).

Diseases, disorders and deficiencies

There are many causes of adverse symptoms in plants. These can be divided into pests, diseases, disorders and deficiencies. In this book, we are dealing with diseases, disorders and deficiencies. Information on controlling fruit and vegetable pests can be found in our companion volume in this series, *How to control Fruit and Vegetable Pests*.

Diseases are caused by parasitic organisms, that is, organisms that live on other forms of life at the expense of their host. Fungi, bacteria and viruses are the main culprits. Disorders and deficiencies, on the other hand, are caused by non-living factors, e.g. poor soil and weather conditions such as frost and drought.

Diseases

In many cases, exact identification of the organism causing a disease is very difficult for the average gardener. Fortunately, to a great extent you can rely on symptoms to tell you the cause of a problem, or you can at least get close enough to make a reasonable decision as to what to do about it.

There is no need, therefore, for all gardeners to have a degree in plant pathology – but it is helpful to learn something about the life history of the disease as this can make any control strategy much more effective and prevent panic setting in!

Typical disease symptoms

Death of tissue – spots.
Abnormal increase in tissue – canker, scab.
Dwarfing or stunting of plants.
Change in colour – yellowing, silvering.
Wilting.
Disintegration of tissue – wet or dry rots.

Some groups of diseases can be found on a wide range of plants, often unrelated. We will deal with these diseases in this section. The more crop specific diseases are covered in the chart on pages 36–59.

Prevention is the best form of disease control. The first part of the book has described how to give plants the growing conditions that they need to grow strongly and vigorously. More specific advice on disease control is given at the end of each disease entry. Infected parts of a plant cannot be 'cured' but there are measures that can be taken to limit further spread.

Fungi

There are around 100,000 species of fungus in Britain alone, mushrooms being the most well known. Unlike green plants, fungi cannot make their own food, so they have to use that already made by other plants. The majority of fungi live on dead and decaying plant material; relatively few feed on living plants, but it is these that cause diseases.

Some parts of a fungus are not visible to the naked eye. At its vegetative stage, the fungus consists of thin strands (hyphae) which grow through, and feed on, the host. It is usually only when a fungus produces its reproductive, or fruiting, bodies that you notice it. These fruiting bodies can range from large toadstools to much smaller, less obvious structures.

Spread
The fruiting bodies produce tiny spores which are blown in the wind, or spread by rain, to infect other parts of the plant, or other plants which may be quite a distance away. The time between initial infection and production of spores can vary drastically, e.g. from a few days in the case of potato blight to several

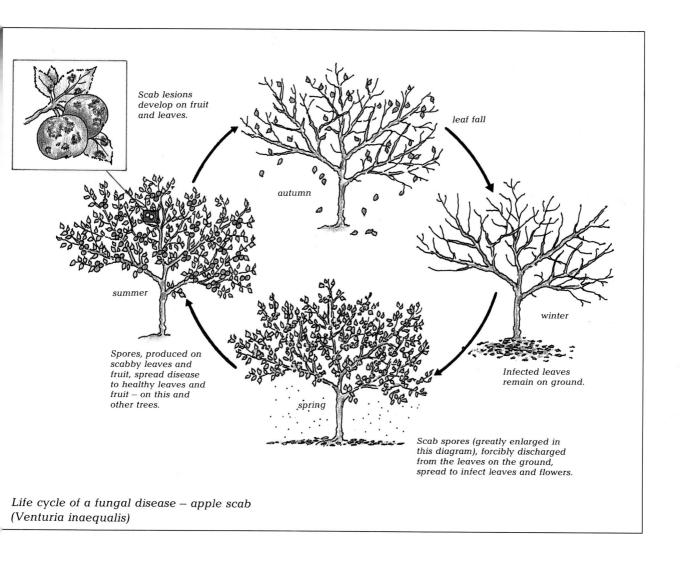

Scab lesions develop on fruit and leaves.

leaf fall

autumn

winter

summer

Infected leaves remain on ground.

Spores, produced on scabby leaves and fruit, spread disease to healthy leaves and fruit — on this and other trees.

spring

Scab spores (greatly enlarged in this diagram), forcibly discharged from the leaves on the ground, spread to infect leaves and flowers.

Life cycle of a fungal disease — apple scab (Venturia inaequalis)

years in the case of silver leaf. Fungi can also spread by other means, e.g. honey fungus grows up to 3 m through the soil in its search for a new host and does not always produce toadstools.

We tend to think of fungal diseases as a problem of damp weather. All need moisture for the spores to grow and infect a plant, but many, such as powdery mildews, are more of a problem in a dry season.

Survival/source of infection

Fungi can survive in various ways even if you think that you have removed all diseased plants. Some may be present, either in other plants of the same type or even in other species, without causing any symptoms. Some will produce special resistant 'resting bodies' which can survive in the soil until another suitable plant comes along. Dead and decaying plant material can also act as a source of infection. Finally, some fungi can survive in seeds and seed tubers.

Host range

Some fungi, such as grey mould, attack plants of many different species. Others limit themselves to a much narrower host range. It is easy to assume that because two different plants have similar symptoms, e.g. rust on leeks and groundsel, that one will pass the disease on to the other. There are, however, many types of rust and the one that troubles groundsel can not infect fruit or vegetables.

General fungal diseases of vegetables

Damping off   Various organisms

Plants affected
Young seedlings of many plants.

Typical symptoms
Seedlings topple over as a result of infection at the stem base. They tend to die out in circular patches. Survivors grow poorly and have wiry stems.

Details
Damping off usually occurs in damp, cold and overcrowded conditions. It is caused by several types of fungi, widespread in garden soils.

Prevention
● Sow seeds thinly into warm soil with a good tilth, so that they germinate quickly.
● Do not overwater.
● Thin as early as possible.

Once infected
● There is no cure.

Damping off on seedlings

Downy mildew   *Peronospora* spp. and other related fungi

Plants affected
Many crops, including brassicas, onions, spinach, beet and lettuce.

Typical symptoms
Yellow patches on the upper surface of leaves, with corresponding patches of off-white/purplish mould underneath, in damp conditions. To distinguish it from the unrelated powdery mildews, wipe off mould. If the leaf underneath is yellow, then it is downy mildew.

Details
Common in cool, damp weather. Caused by several different species of fungus, each of which is only able to attack one group of plants, e.g. the crucifer family. Within each species of fungus there may be different strains which can infect only one plant species.

Downy mildew on brassicas (*Peronospora parasitica*) may kill young seedlings. This mildew may also infect watercress and wallflowers. Both seedlings and mature lettuce plants are open to infection from lettuce downy mildew (*Bremia lactucae*) which weakens them and paves the way for grey mould. Other strains of *Bremia* also attack chicory and endive. Onion downy mildew (*Peronospora destructor*) can be a severe problem and is one of the causes of bulbs rotting in store. Seeds saved from infected plants will grow poorly. Other mildews that can be a problem include *Peronospora farinosa*, different strains of which attack the beet family and spinach. *Peronospora nivea* attacks celery and parsnips, whilst *Peronospora viciae*, attacks peas and, sometimes, broad beans.

Downy mildew fungi can survive in the form of resting bodies; in the soil, in dead and dying crops, and in crop debris. They can also exist in seemingly healthy plants, e.g. overwintering onions can harbour downy mildew which will be able to infect the new spring-sown crop.

Once plants are infected, the disease can spread very rapidly in cool, damp weather. The spores are spread by wind and rain.

Prevention

● Use a 5 year rotation, especially where downy mildew has occurred.

● Thin seedlings early and space wide apart to allow good air flow.

● Clear up at the end of the season.

● Break the cycle, see pages 13, 16–17.

Once infected

● Remove infected plants; do not compost them.

● For spray details, see pages 60–61.

Downy mildew on lettuce

Powdery mildew *Erysiphe cichoracearum* and *Sphaerotheca fuliginea*

Plants affected

Brassicas, courgettes, cucumbers and peas are the most commonly affected.

Typical symptoms

White powdery coating on almost any part of the plant. Individual off-white patches appear which may spread to cover the whole plant. Infected parts may be distorted and discoloured and the whole plant weakened.

Details

Common when it is warm and dry during the day and cold at night, and on dry soils.

There are many different powdery mildew fungi, each of which infects specific types of plant. This is complicated by the fact that one

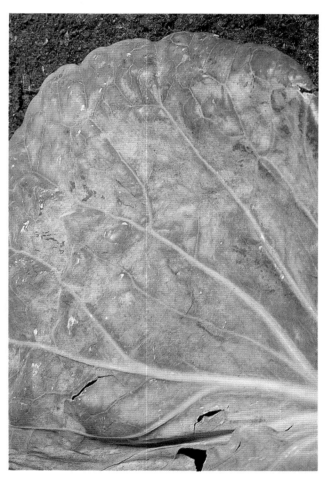

Powdery mildew on brassica

plant may be susceptible to more than one type of powdery mildew.

Crucifer mildew (*Erysiphe cruciferarum*) is a particular problem of swedes and turnips, but can also infect any of the cabbage family, related ornamentals such as wallflowers and unrelated ones such as poppies (*Papaver* spp.). Pea mildew (*Erysiphe pisi*) will also infect lupins and tares (green manures).

Mildew on outdoor courgettes, cucumbers and pumpkins often occurs late in the season when the vigour of the plants is declining. It causes little problem then.

Powdery mildew on marrow

Most powdery mildews survive on crop debris but pea mildew may be carried in the seed. See also apple and gooseberry mildew, pages 50–51, 56–57.

Prevention
● Ensure that plants are not short of water, see pages 6–7.
● Sow turnips and swedes late, and peas early, to avoid dry periods.
● Grow mildew-resistant varieties.
● Clear up at the end of the season.
● Use wider spacing between plants.

Once infected
● Remove infected plants; do not compost them.
● Break the cycle, see pages 13, 16–17.
● For spray details, see pages 60–61.

Foot and root rots
Plants affected
Asparagus, lettuce, peas, beans and tomatoes are the most commonly affected.

Typical symptoms
The plant rots at ground level. The earliest symptoms are stunting of plants which turn yellow and wilt, often very suddenly. They differ from true wilts in that there is no discolouration in the stem.

Details
Caused by several soil-living fungi. Most can only enter a plant through a small wound. They are more common in plants under stress.

Prevention
● Create good growing conditions for plants, see pages 4–15.
● Avoid excessive or insufficient watering.
● Use a crop rotation.

Once infected
● Stop watering.
● Encourage new roots by earthing up stems of tomato plants that have not collapsed.
● Dig up infected plants; do not compost them.
● Increase rotation of peas to at least 5 years.

Sclerotinia *Sclerotinia sclerotiorum*
Plants affected
Widespread, infecting many types of vegetables and ornamentals. Vegetables most commonly infected include beans, celery, cucurbits, lettuce, peas, potatoes and tomatoes. Can also appear on the crown of carrots and parsnip roots in store.

Typical symptoms
The first sign is often when plants wilt suddenly and topple over. A wet, brown rot, sometimes with a white cottony mould, will be found at the base of the stem. Large black resting bodies, up to 1 cm long, can be found within the stem or in the white mould.

Details
Most common in damp, cool regions. The resting bodies survive in the soil and in crop

Sclerotinia on peas

debris, and act as a source of infection, usually through a wound.

Prevention
- Crop rotation.
- Avoid damp spots.
- Allow adequate space between plants.

Once infected
- Remove infected plants; do not compost them.
- In store, check and remove infected roots to prevent spread.
- Increase length of rotation.

Violet root rot *Helicobasidium brebissonii*

Plants affected
Carrots, beetroot, parsnips, potatoes, swedes, turnips, seakale, asparagus and celery are the most seriously attacked.

Typical symptoms
A colourful disease. Infected plants may grow poorly; the roots develop a coating of purple strands to which soil sticks. There may be some rot under the purple coat and large black resting bodies may be seen.

Details
Most common in wet soils and in acid conditions. The disease is slow to spread and symptoms often do not appear until late in the season. In the absence of a host plant, the resting bodies of the fungus can survive in the soil for many years. They just wait for the right host to arrive.

Prevention
- Correct pH and drainage if necessary.
- Crop rotation.
- Maintain good soil fertility.

Once infected
- Remove infected plants; do not compost.
- Do not grow susceptible crops for 3 to 4 years. Crops that *do not* get violet root rot are Brussels sprouts, cabbage, cauliflower, peas and corn.

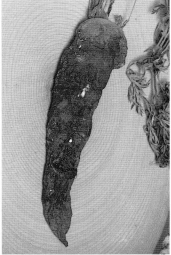

Violet root rot and the affect of violet root rot on carrot

Wilts *Fusarium* and *Verticillium* spp.

Plants affected
Peas, beans, cucurbits and tomatoes are the most commonly affected.

Typical symptoms
Symptoms, which appear on older leaves first, include wilting. At first, they will often recover at night. Leaf stalks may bend down. There is a characteristic brown stain in the stem when cut well above ground level. Symptoms may be one-sided. There is no rotting.

Wilt on peas

Details
Several soil-living fungi are responsible for true wilt diseases. The fungus that attacks peas and beans is specific to them; others are indiscriminate. Wilts are worse in poor growing conditions and can survive in the soil for several years without a suitable host.

Prevention
● Good growing conditions.
● Crop rotation.
● Resistant varieties.

Once infected
● Dig up infected plants; do not compost them.
● Follow an infected crop with one that is not susceptible, e.g. carrots, parsnips, celery.
● Increase rotation to 6 years.

General fungal diseases of fruit

Coral spot *Nectria cinnabarina*

Plants affected
Currants, gooseberries and apples; also other woody plants.

Typical symptoms
Pink pustules on dead twigs or branches; branches may die back.

Details
Spores are carried on wind and enter through dead branches or twigs or other wounds, e.g. bad pruning, mechanical or frost damage, low branch smothered by tall weeds. Fungus can move into living tissue, causing wilting of leaves and death of branch or whole plant (some strains more vigorous than others). Pink pustules (sometimes red in spring) appear after infection and release spores.

Prevention
● Do not leave piles of dead branches or old pea-sticks near growing fruit.
● Prune carefully.
● Remove all frosted or damaged tissue.
● Inspect plants regularly.

Once infected
● Prune out at first signs of pustules, cutting back at least 15 cm into healthy wood. Burn infected wood immediately and disinfect secateurs.

Coral spot

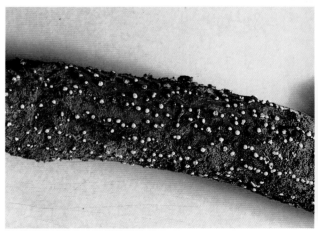

Grey mould *Botrytis cinerea*

Plants affected

Flowers of blackcurrants, fruits of strawberries, raspberries, blackberries, gooseberries and currants, and branches of gooseberries and currants.

Typical symptoms

Flowers: not apparent until later in season when death of flowers is revealed by a poor crop. (This could have other causes.)
Fruits: become rotten; grey fluffy mould spreads over rotted area.
Branches: suddenly die back with no other symptoms.

Details

A very prevalent fungus with many hosts. Most common in damp, cool conditions. Enters currant blossoms in early spring and works up the truss so that few flowers are pollinated. Later fruits of many crops may be attacked if the weather stays damp. Particularly common on strawberries which spread infection one to another as they touch. Grey fluffy mould develops, releasing clouds of spores when touched. Infection initiated through petals, bruises or wounds. The same fungus also causes sudden die-back of branches in gooseberries and currants, often with no other apparent symptoms.

Prevention

● Allow proper spacing between plants.

● Protect strawberries with cloches in cool, wet weather.

● The early varieties and early-flowering varieties are more likely to be susceptible.

Once infected

● No cure for blossom damage.

● Pick over soft fruit crops regularly to remove any mouldy fruits.

● Cut out whole branches affected by die-back and burn them. If the disease persists or whole bushes are affected, then dig up and burn the whole plant.

Remarks

Disease is not soil-borne and new stock may be planted where currants or gooseberries were grubbed out.

Toadstools of honey fungus. Carefully check your fruit trees and shrubs if you find these in your garden.

Honey fungus *Armillaria mellea*

Plants affected

All woody fruit types; woody and some herbaceous ornamentals.

Typical symptoms

Creeping death across patch of garden or trees/bushes dying in succession. Branches die back; bark near base of stem pulls away easily, revealing white sheets smelling of mushrooms.

Details

A serious disease affecting a wide range of plants and spreading from plant to plant up to 1.5 m every year. After initial symptoms, see above, plants die and roots decay. Black 'bootlace' strands (rhizomorphs) initiate from the base of the plant and head off through the soil to find new hosts. Toadstools appear round the base in autumn, varying in colour from grey/pink to honey yellow. Accurate diagnosis is not easy as early signs and symptoms are not always obvious. Spreads by root contact and, most importantly, rhizomorphs.

Prevention

● Do not leave old tree stumps in the ground. Large stumps can be removed by a contractor

23

with a special grinding machine. Killing stumps chemically is not sufficient.

● Do not grow fruit trees or bushes on sites known to be infected. Strawberries are not usually affected.

● The use of bark mulches is not likely to spread honey fungus.

Once infected

● Remove and burn affected plants.

● Try to find as many 'bootlace' strands as possible.

● To clear a site of infection do not replant susceptible plants. Amongst the most susceptible are apple, birch, cedar, cypress, lilac, pine, privet, walnut and willow. Without a host the fungus will eventually die out.

Sooty mould *Cladosporium* spp. and others

Plants affected
All fruits.

Typical symptoms
Black sticky mould covers leaves and fruits.

Details
Fungus grows on sticky 'honeydew' excreted by sap-sucking insects, such as aphids. Gives appearance of plant covered in soot. Does not directly harm plant or fruit but can reduce ability of leaves to photosynthesise and may even cause them to fall early. Fouling on fruit is easily wiped off.

Prevention
● Keep insect pests under control.

Once infected
● Rainfall will wash some off. Wash or wipe 'sooty' fruits.

Storage rots *Penicillium* spp., *Sclerotinia fructigena* and others

Plants affected
Stored apples and pears.

Typical symptoms
Fruits rot. Other symptoms may vary considerably.

Storage rot on apple

Details
Variety in symptoms results from attack by different fungi, including some that affect growing fruit, e.g. brown rot, see pages 50–51, and grey mould, see page 23. In all cases, rotting will be apparent and individual symptoms are unimportant. Some disorders also affect stored fruit but do not usually cause rotting, see bitter pit, pages 52–53.

Prevention
● Inspect stored fruit regularly.

● Do not store damaged or diseased fruits.

● Store carefully on open slatted trays, either individually wrapped in newspaper or waxed paper, or unwrapped but not touching.

● Apples can be stored in plastic bags with pinhole perforations – this can occasionally cause a disorder from scalding by natural gases (dark staining around 'eye').

● In all cases, fruit store should be cool but frost-free, dark and well ventilated but not too dry.

Once infected
● Remove rotten fruits and compost them.

Bacteria

Bacteria are extremely simple organisms. They are single cells that multiply by dividing into identical single cells. They cannot be seen by the naked eye and rely on living plants or animals for their existence. There are comparatively few bacterial diseases of plants; blackleg of potatoes and bacterial canker on plums are two examples.

Bacteria are spread in the soil water, and scattered by wind and rain; some are spread in and on seed and planting material. The majority of bacteria can only infect through a wound, caused by a pest or heavy handling, because they cannot break through a plant's protective skin.

Typical bacterial symptoms are a softening of the tissues, that is, rotting (some fungi cause rots too) and a nasty smell.

Details of all the bacterial diseases covered in this book can be found in the chart on pages 36–59.

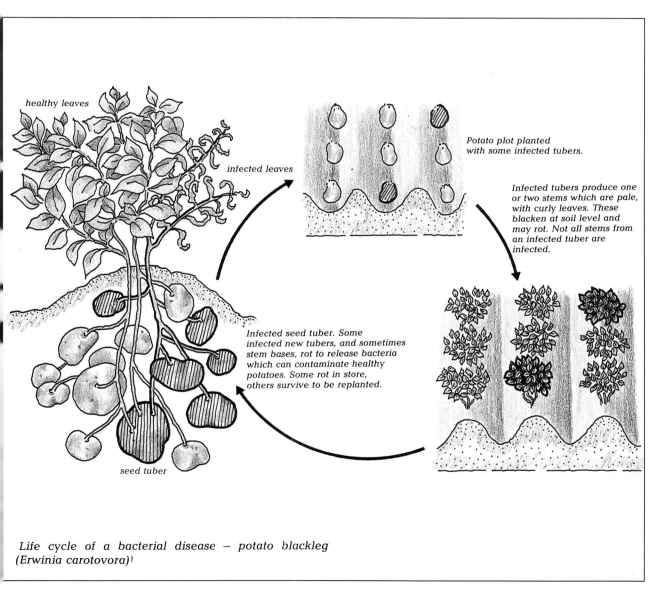

healthy leaves

infected leaves

Potato plot planted with some infected tubers.

Infected tubers produce one or two stems which are pale, with curly leaves. These blacken at soil level and may rot. Not all stems from an infected tuber are infected.

Infected seed tuber. Some infected new tubers, and sometimes stem bases, rot to release bacteria which can contaminate healthy potatoes. Some rot in store, others survive to be replanted.

seed tuber

Life cycle of a bacterial disease – potato blackleg (Erwinia carotovora)[1]

Viruses

Viruses are much smaller than bacteria. They are only a few hundred thousandths of a centimetre long and are so basic that they can only multiply by using the mechanism in the cells of other organisms. Despite their size, they are responsible for some of the most destructive of plant diseases – stunting growth and reducing cropping dramatically.

It is impossible for the average gardener to identify a virus precisely and, even if you can, there is no cure. The important thing is to be sure that it *is* a virus, so that you can take appropriate action.

There are many viruses, which cause a whole host of symptoms, including stunted growth, malformations, and mottled and mosaic patterns on leaves. It is beyond the scope of this book to describe them all. We have just included the most common.

The symptoms of viral infections are easily confused with those caused by mineral deficiencies, see pages 31–35, or those caused by the environment, such as drought or frost, see pages 28–30. However, disorders and deficiencies would affect a whole row or batch of plants, whilst a virus will often only affect individual plants. Viral symptoms may come and go, and can vanish in hot weather. The best time to look for them is on cool, dull days.

Some viruses are plant specific. Others will infect a number of unrelated plants. They are not necessarily confined to the plants after which they have been named.

Viruses generally survive in living plant

Life cycle of a viral disease – blackcurrant reversion

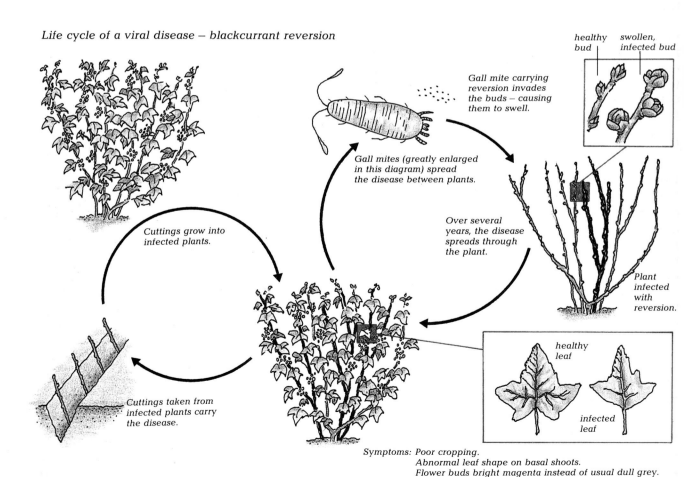

healthy bud

swollen, infected bud

Gall mite carrying reversion invades the buds – causing them to swell.

Gall mites (greatly enlarged in this diagram) spread the disease between plants.

Cuttings grow into infected plants.

Over several years, the disease spreads through the plant.

Plant infected with reversion.

Cuttings taken from infected plants carry the disease.

healthy leaf

infected leaf

Symptoms: Poor cropping.
Abnormal leaf shape on basal shoots.
Flower buds bright magenta instead of usual dull grey.

A virus on turnip

A virus on brassica

material, where they can lurk without showing any symptoms. They are spread by aphids and other sap-sucking insects, by contact (contaminated hands, secateurs), by birds, in soil and by propagating from contaminated plants (cuttings, budding, grafting). Knowing the method of spread can help in controlling the problem.

Dealing with viruses

Viruses can infect a wide range of plants, causing a multitude of symptoms, but the action that can be taken to deal with them is, more or less, common to all. For this reason, the 'prevention' and 'once infected' details are given here.

Symptoms and details of viruses affecting specific crops are given in the chart on pages 36–59.

Prevention

● Control of the creature that passes on the virus may help in some cases.

● Grow resistant varieties.

● Remove alternative hosts if there is a recurring problem (break the cycle).

● Rotation.

● Buy planting material that is certified virus-free.

A virus on onion

● Never use seed saved from diseased plants.

● Replace strawberry plants every 3 years; do not save your own runners.

Once infected

● Dig up infected plants and remove from the garden. There is no cure. Even if effects are confined to part of a plant, the virus is likely to have invaded the whole system.

27

Disorders

Adverse environmental conditions, such as low temperatures, frost, wind, a variable water supply, drought, and even heavy-handed gardening, can cause unusual symptoms in growing plants, which may at times be confused with pest or disease damage. Such symptoms are known as disorders.

General disorders of vegetables

Bolting

Bolting is when plants run to flower prematurely. It can be caused by a variety of factors. Once a plant has bolted there is no remedy, but there are ways of ensuring that it does not happen in the first place.

Beetroot/spinach beet. Low temperatures will cause early crops to bolt; choose a bolt-resistant beetroot variety; sow spinach beet later.

Celery and celeriac. Both are very sensitive to cold. Minimum temperature should be around 12°C; remember that this applies also when plants are being hardened off. Do not plant out too early. If the weather delays transplanting, then clip back plants to a height of 6 cm or so.

Chinese cabbage. Seedlings and plants subjected to temperatures below 10°C will be stimulated to flower. The long days of summer also encourage flowering. Sow as directed on packet – often not until mid-June, or later.

Spinach. The long days of summer, when it can be light for over 13 hours, encourage spinach to flower. Grow it during the shorter days of autumn, winter and spring.

Onions. Overwintering varieties will go to flower if too large. Smaller plants will not respond to the cold stimulus. Timing of sowing is critical. In the UK the following are suggested: South – last week August; Midlands – mid-August; North and Scotland – first week August. Make sure that they really get going when they are sown and that the soil is not too dry for germination.

Bolting brassica

Spring cabbage. Will bolt early if too large over winter, so do not sow too early.

Very dry conditions will also encourage plants to bolt, especially celery, celeriac and onions. See pages 5–6, 13 for information on moisture holding.

No fruit setting

Outdoor cucurbit flowers must be pollinated in order to get fruit. Early in the season, lack of setting may be due to absence of pollen, if male and female flowers were not open at the same time. Bad weather may also inhibit the activity of the pollinating insects. A shortage of water can prevent fruit forming.

Runner beans (*Phaseolus coccineus*) may also fail to set at times. A shortage of water, excessive temperatures or a shortage of pollinating insects are the usual causes.

Splitting

Splitting is caused by irregular water supply, often when water is applied after a long dry period, causing rapid growth. Improve the water-holding capacity of the soil to reduce the likelihood of this happening, see pages 5–6, 13.

Split carrot

Frost damage

Frost damage will appear overnight. It is often mistaken for some disease or blight. Leaves wilt or shrivel, or may just go brown at the edges. They do not usually fall. Several unrelated crops may be affected in the same area. Frost may damage mature crops at the end of the season if they are left in too long, e.g. summer cabbages. A severe frost after a very mild autumn can, surprisingly, kill plants which are normally hardy, such as broccoli and other brassicas.

Prevention
● See page 10.

Frost damage on potato

Herbicide damage

Plants can be damaged by herbicides, either when spray drifts on to them, in which case the damage is death of parts or all of the plant, or by hormone herbicide residues in straw. Cucumbers and tomatoes are particularly susceptible to hormone herbicide damage, distorting plants, causing narrowing of leaves, and stunting. Brassicas may also be affected.

Prevention
● Obtain straw from organic farms.

Oedema

Rough, warty outgrowths develop on undersides of leaves and on stems of brassicas. These are caused by an excess of water in the plant. The problem should fade when humidity falls, or when watering is reduced.

General disorders of fruit

Bruised or marked fruit
Hail damage will ruin soft-skinned fruits and may allow brown rot or other fungi to penetrate. Brown spot marking or lines on one side of mature apples or pear skins may be the result of a spring hailstorm. If fruit is insufficiently thinned, then wind can also cause bruising.

Fruit splitting
Sudden changes in water availability, when heavy rain follows a drought, causes fruit skins, and sometimes bark, to split. To avoid this problem, see 'problems with water', pages 4–7.

Wilting of leaves
This is not always caused by a disease. Lack of water could be the culprit. Initial symptoms of frost will also cause wilting. To avoid this, see 'problems with water', pages 4–7, and also 'death of flowers', below.

Broken branches, twigs and canes
Clumsy gardeners break branches and so does the wind. Quite often, a good year provides a very heavy crop and if this is not sufficiently thinned, then its weight may break a branch. Plums are especially prone and branches may need propping up if crops are heavy.

Such damage allows entry of disease if it is not pruned out. To avoid it, protect crop from wind, see pages 7 and 10, thin fruit, tie in raspberry canes and prop up heavily laden branches.

Death of flowers, young leaves or shoots
If this happens early in the year, then the most likely cause is frost damage. If frost is severe, then whole shoots may be killed, or, in the case of cane fruits, young emerging canes. Early-flowering varieties, and all plums, pears and cherries, are susceptible to frost. To avoid frost damage, see page 10.

Bad pruning cuts, see pages 12–13, can leave a snag and the branch dies back.

Blossom wilt, wither tip, see page 10,

56–57, and cankers may follow frost or other damage. Prune out or pick off affected parts.

Death of bushes or trees
Honey fungus is not the only killer. Used carelessly, strimmers, mowers and hoes can cut so much bark that the bush or tree no longer has a sap flow. The result is death. Smaller wounds invite diseases.

Excessive growth: poor fruiting
Vigorous growth is quite desirable in a young plant, but not in older plants as it may reduce fruit production, shade maturing fruit, make picking awkward and provide better conditions for fungal spores to find a home.

Hard pruning in winter leads to vigorous growth. Careful summer pruning will moderate vigour. Bad planting, see page 12, can lead to trees rooting above the graft mark and growing on their own roots. This can result in over-vigorous growth.

Overfeeding can encourage lush growth at the expense of fruit. Such growth is more prone to disease and wind damage.

Poor cropping
Excessive vigour, see above, frost damage, see page 10, and poor weather conditions at pollination time, see pages 9–10, will all reduce cropping.

Frost damage on raspberry

Mineral deficiencies

Poor growth and a variety of, often colourful, leaf symptoms can be caused by a shortage of one or more plant foods. This is known as a mineral deficiency. It may be due to a shortage of a particular nutrient in the soil, or due to that nutrient being present but unavailable to the plant.

Shortage of water, an excess of another nutrient, or an adverse pH can all make nutrients unavailable.

Identifying the problem

General mineral deficiency symptoms are given here. More specific crop symptoms can be found in the chart, see pages 36–59. These symptoms are quite easily confused with those from other causes, including virus infection or root damage, so do not make a snap diagnosis.

> **Hints and tips for identifying mineral deficiencies**
>
> ● Note where the symptoms appear first – on the new leaves, the old leaves, or all over?
>
> ● Note the pattern of any colouration/ yellowing – is it between the veins, around the edges, or all over? If the veins only are yellow, then it is *not* a deficiency.
>
> ● If there is more than one plant, then note the distribution of the symptoms through the crop. In a small area, such as a vegetable bed, all the plants of the same type are likely to be affected in the same way, to the same extent, though plants at the edges may be less affected. Variations may be seen if parts of the plot were treated differently in past years.
>
> ● A soil analysis can help to confirm the diagnosis, identifying basic deficiencies in the soil and problems caused by pH and overfeeding.

General causes and cures

Once a plant is showing deficiency symptoms it is likely that yields will be reduced for that season. The best solution to mineral deficiencies, and to the problem of identifying them correctly, is to avoid them in the first place. Follow the guidelines for creating a healthy soil, see page 4, and refer also to the companion handbook in this series, *Soil Care and Management* by Jo Readman.

> **Causes and cures**
>
> ● Heavy soils are rarely short of plant foods, but they are not always available to the plants. Improving the structure will increase fertility.
>
> ● Light soils quickly lose plant foods. Improve structure and grow green manures over winter to reduce loss of foods.
>
> ● A cold snap that checks plant growth can cause short-term deficiencies which will disappear when the weather changes.
>
> ● A water shortage may not allow a plant to take up enough food. Increase watering and improve soil structure.
>
> ● If uncomposted, tough organic material, such as fresh straw or wood shavings, is added to the soil, then the bacteria which normally help to decompose it will use the nitrogen in the soil. This 'nitrogen robbery' means that there is little left over for growing plants. In time it will be made available again, but this can take years in the case of wood shavings.
>
> ● If the soil is basically short of a mineral, then this can be added, see individual entries on the following pages. Liquid feeds may be used as a short-term solution, followed by longer term measures. The plant foods in a liquid feed are immediately available to the growing plant and do not contribute to the health of the soil – which means that they do not fulfil the basic requirements of an organic fertiliser.
>
> ● Overliming or overfeeding can cause a shortage by making other nutrients unavailable.

General deficiencies

Boron (B) deficiency

Plants most commonly affected

VEGETABLES: Beetroot, carrots, celery, cauliflowers, tomatoes.

FRUIT: Pears.

Typical symptoms

Distortion, blackening or death of young growing points. Leaves flag, with a yellow or scorched look, and go brittle. Fruit tree bark has rough and pimpled appearance. Can be confused with stem eelworm or herbicide damage.

Details

A true boron deficiency is most likely on granite and light sandy soils. Boron may be present, but unavailable, in soils with a high pH. May be worse in wet seasons.

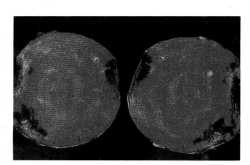

Boron deficiency in beetroot

Boron deficiency in broccoli

What can be done?

FOR QUICK EFFECT:
- Add Borax, at 3 g per sq m.

MEDIUM/LONG-TERM:
- Avoid overliming and overfeeding with nitrogen, both of which can encourage boron deficiency in a plant.

Calcium (Ca) deficiency

Plants most commonly affected

VEGETABLES: Brussels sprouts, celery, cabbages, lettuce, tomatoes.

FRUIT: Apples (see bitter pit, pages 52–53).

Typical symptoms

Cupping and scorching of leaves, youngest leaves first. Disorders in heart of leafy vegetables, roots and fruits. Can be confused with frost or herbicide damage.

Calcium deficiency in Brussels sprouts

Details

A calcium deficiency in plants is usually due to restricted uptake rather than a shortage in the soil. Can be caused by lack of water or excessive use of potassium or magnesium fertilisers.

What can be done?

FOR QUICK EFFECT:
- Improve water supply if drought is cause.

LONG-TERM:
- Improve water-holding capacity of soil, see pages 5–6.

- Lime, to raise pH if it is low.
- Stop using potassium fertilisers if analysis shows that levels are high.

Iron (Fe) deficiency

Plants most commonly affected

VEGETABLES: Rare.

FRUIT: Apples, plums, pears, raspberries.

Typical symptoms

Leaves yellow between veins, or all over, youngest first. They may have a bleached look. Branches die back; fruit has good colour.

Details

A deficiency in the soil is rare. Iron can be unavailable to plants if the pH is high, if the soil has been overfertilised with phosphorus, or if it is waterlogged. Can be confused with manganese deficiency.

What can be done?

- Correct soil problems.

Iron deficiency in tomato

Magnesium (Mg) deficiency

Plants most commonly affected

VEGETABLES: Potatoes, tomatoes.

FRUIT: Apples, blackcurrants, gooseberries, raspberries.

Typical symptoms

Yellowing between leaf veins giving a marbled effect. Red pigmented plants may show brilliant tints. Fruits small and woody. Symptoms show on oldest leaves first, from end of June. Can be confused with virus, or natural ageing of lower tomato leaves.

Details

Magnesium is easily washed out, so it is more common on light soils and in wet seasons. Excessive use of potassium fertilisers can make magnesium unavailable to plants.

What can be done?

FOR QUICK EFFECT:

- Foliar feed fortnightly, with a 2% solution of 10% Epsom salts.

LONG-TERM:

- Reduce use of potassium fertilisers if this is a cause.
- Add dolomite limestone if pH of soil allows.

Magnesium deficiency in tomato

Magnesium deficiency in carrot

33

Manganese (Mn) deficiency

Plants most commonly affected

VEGETABLES: Peas, French beans, onions.

FRUIT: Apples, cherries, raspberries.

Typical symptoms

Leaves yellow between veins and patches may die off, youngest leaves first. Symptoms can spread quickly, and the plant may grow away from the problem so that new leaves may seem less affected. Can be confused with iron or magnesium deficiency.

Details

A manganese soil deficiency is most common in poorly drained soils and in those high in organic matter. It may be unavailable to plants where pH is high.

What can be done?

LONG-TERM:
- Do not overlime.
- Improve soil structure.

Nitrogen deficiency in potato

Nitrogen deficiency in strawberry

Manganese deficiency in French beans

Nitrogen deficiency in onion

Nitrogen (N) deficiency

Plants most commonly affected

VEGETABLES: All except peas and beans.

FRUIT: Apples, plums, currants.

Typical symptoms

Poor growth; leaves pale and may show red and purple tints, oldest leaves first. Fruits small and highly coloured, with sweet taste.

Can be confused with root damage, drought or phosphorus deficiency.

Details
Most common in light soils and those low in organic matter. Also in neglected orchards. Low temperatures and 'nitrogen robbery' can cause temporary deficiency.

What can be done?
Nitrogen is found in plant and animal remains, such as animal manures and garden compost. It is not, like the other plant foods, a constituent of the rocks from which the soil is formed.

FOR QUICK EFFECT:
● Water, or foliar feed with a liquid manure.

MEDIUM-TERM:
● Mulch with grass mowings, animal manures or compost.
● Feed soil with hoof and horn, or blood, fish and bone meal.

LONG-TERM:
● Improve soil structure and fertility, see page 4.
● Grow green manures over winter to reduce loss through leaching.
● Grow nitrogen-fixing green manures to increase nitrogen in the soil.

Phosphorus (P) deficiency

Plants most commonly affected
VEGETABLES: Seedlings, carrots, lettuce, spinach.
FRUIT: Apples, blackcurrants, gooseberries.

Typical symptoms
Poor growth, especially in young plants. Leaves may turn blue/green or purplish but not yellow; oldest leaves first. May fall early. Fruits small and green with acid taste. Can be confused with virus, drought, root damage or nitrogen deficiency.

Details
Most common in acid soils, especially in areas of high rainfall. Also in clay and poor chalk soils. Cold weather can cause temporary deficiency.

What can be done?
MEDIUM-TERM:
● Add bone meal or bone flour.

LONG-TERM:
● Add rock phosphate.

Potassium (K) deficiency

Plants most commonly affected
VEGETABLES: Potatoes, tomatoes.
FRUIT: Apples, currants, gooseberries.

Typical symptoms
Brown scorching on tips and edges of leaves, which may curl up. Yellowing between veins, oldest leaves first. Fruits drop and may be small, woody and sweet. Can be confused with wind scorch and drought.

Details
Most common in light sandy soils, and chalky or peaty soils with a low clay content. Also in heavy soils with poor structure.

What can be done?
FOR QUICK EFFECT:
● Feed with home-made comfrey liquid manure.

MEDIUM-TERM:
● Feed with seaweed meal.

LONG-TERM:
● Improve soil structure.

Potassium deficiency in French beans

Crop by crop — diseases, disorders & deficiencies at a glance

	TYPICAL SYMPTOMS	CAUSE	DETAILS
Seedlings	Seedlings of many crops collapse; stem base decayed and/or grey mould present. Any survivors grow poorly.	**Damping off** Various fungi Fungal disease	The diseases that cause damping off are common in most soils and are most of a problem in cold, overcrowded conditions.
Asparagus	Plants die back; base of stem and/or roots rot.	**Foot and root rots** Fungal disease	See page 20.
	Plants feeble and stunted; matted dark strands on roots.	**Violet root rot** *Helicobasidium brebissonii* Fungal disease	See page 21.
	Shoots blacken and die suddenly in spring.	**Frost** Disorder	See pages 9–10, 28–30.
	Rusty coloured powdery pustules on leaves, darker streaks on stems. Shoots may die.	**Asparagus rust** *Puccinia asparagi* Fungal disease	Survives the winter as resting spores in the soil; also on crop debris.
Beans and Peas	BEANS AND PEAS Foliage discolours and plants wilt. Roots and/or stem base rots.	**Foot and root rots** Fungal disease	See page 20.
	Stems rot at base; white cottony mould present.	**Sclerotinia** *Sclerotinia sclerotiorum* Fungal disease	See pages 20–21.
	Leaves show yellow mosaic pattern. Leaflets curl down. Plants stunted, bushy; pods distorted.	**Bean yellow mosaic** Viral disease	The main source of this aphid-spread virus is red clover and gladioli.
	Leaves with marked yellowing between the veins; edges remain green.	**Magnesium deficiency**	See page 33.
	Leaves with scorched tips and edges, oldest first. Edges may curl.	**Potassium deficiency**	See page 35.
	Plants wilt, oldest leaves first. Dark streaks in stems when cut through.	**Wilt** Fungal disease	See page 22.
	BROAD BEANS ONLY Small chocolate-brown spots on upper surface of leaves and on stems. In damp conditions, spots may merge and blacken.	**Chocolate spot** *Botrytis fabae* Fungal disease	Source of disease can be crop debris, other broad beans, winter tares and field beans.
	Upper part of plant turns yellow; leaves thicken and become brittle. Plants stunted.	**Pea leaf roll** Viral disease	Spread by aphids.
	Stems thin, lower leaves drop early.	**Phosphorus deficiency**	See page 35.

PREVENTION	ONCE INFECTED	REMARKS
Sow seeds thinly into warm soil so they grow quickly. Do not use collected rainwater for seedlings.		
See page 20.	See page 20.	
See page 21.	See page 21.	Less common in northern areas.
See pages 7, 9–10.	Nothing can be done.	
Grow asparagus in a well-ventilated site. Clear up crop debris at end of season.	Cut back infected feathery shoots as soon as noticed. Burn or dispose of outside the garden. Dust with sulphur, see page 61.	Can reduce crop.
See page 20.	See page 20. For peas, increase rotation to 5 years.	
See pages 20–21.		
See pages 26–27.	See pages 26–27.	
See page 33.	See page 33.	
See page 35.	See page 35.	
See page 22.	See page 22.	
Avoid damp, sheltered sites. Increase soil potash levels if low. Crop rotation. Break the cycle of infection, see pages 13, 17.	Clear up and compost crop debris.	Autumn-sown beans are more prone to infection.
Good aphid control can limit the problem. See also pages 26–27.	See pages 26–27.	
See page 35.	See page 35.	

Damping off on seedlings that have been allowed to overgrow

Broad beans with rust (speckled dots) and onset of chocolate spot (larger blotches)

Rust on broad beans

Beans and Peas continued

BROAD BEANS; PEAS
Rusty-brown pustules on under-sides of leaves and on stems.

Rust
Uromyces fabae
Fungal disease

Spectacular but rarely serious.

Leaves with yellowish patches on upper surface and white mould beneath in damp weather.

Downy mildew
Peronospora viciae
Fungal disease

See pages 18–19.

FRENCH AND RUNNER BEANS
Small, angular, water-soaked spots, with a yellow/green halo, on leaves. Pods may show greasy spots.

Halo blight
Pseudomonas syringae pv. phaseolicola
Bacterial disease

Infected seed is a main source of disease, which is spread between plants by rain splash and wind.

Light mosaic pattern on leaves. No symptoms on pods.

Bean common mosaic
Viral disease

Spread by aphids; also in seed.

RUNNER BEANS
Flowers fail to set pods.

Various disorders

See pages 28–30.

PEAS
Severe crinkling and mottling of leaves. Pods rough and crinkly.

Pea enation virus

Good aphid control can limit spread. See also pages 26–27.

Yellow-brown, sometimes sunken, spots with pale centre and dark margin – on leaves, stems and pods.

Pea leaf and pod spot
Aschochyta pisi
Fungal disease

Seedlings may be killed; older plants crop poorly, producing blackened or rotting peas. Infected seed and crop debris are main source of infection.

Leaves and pods with white powdery patches, especially on late sowings.

Powdery mildew
Erysiphe pisi
Fungal disease

May also attack tares and alfalfa (green manures).

Beetroot and Spinach Beet

Small circular spots – pale grey with purple-brown margins – on leaves.

Beet leaf spot
Cercospora beticola
Fungal disease

Source of disease can be infected seed, crop debris and other infected plants. More common in damp weather.

Leaves pale and toughened or with pale patches. Grey mould on under surface in damp weather.

Downy mildew
Peronospora farinosa
Fungal disease

See pages 18–19.

Leaves mottled and distorted; veins clear. Plant may be stunted.

Beet mosaic
Viral disease

Spread by aphids but controlling them has little effect. See also pages 26–27.

Leaves yellow between the veins, oldest first. Edges may roll upwards.

Manganese deficiency

See page 34.

Flowering stems produced prematurely.

Bolting
Disorder

Low temperatures will cause early crops to bolt.

Roots with rough patches on surface; dark patches or rings in flesh.

Boron deficiency

See page 32.

BEETROOT
Outer leaves thicken, show abnormal colours, and become dry and brittle.

Beet yellows
Viral disease

Rapid aphid control can keep it in check. See also pages 26–27.

PREVENTION	ONCE INFECTED	REMARKS
Avoid damp, sheltered sites.	Clear up and compost crop debris.	Looks much worse than it is.
See pages 18–19.	See pages 18–19.	More common on peas than broad beans.
Do not use seed from infected plants. Do not soak seeds together in water before sowing – mix them with damp compost instead.	Remove infected plants. Bordeaux mixture can be used to restrict spread, but do not use after first small pods formed, see page 61.	
See pages 26–27.	See pages 26–27.	
See pages 28–30.	See pages 28–30.	
See pages 26–27.	See pages 26–27.	
Do not use seed from an infected crop. Crop rotation. Avoid damp sites.	Remove infected plants and dispose of them outside the garden.	May also infect tares and sweet peas.
See pages 19–20.	See pages 19–20.	
Clear up crop debris. Use wide row spacings. Break the cycle. Never use seed from infected plants.	Pick off infected leaves to reduce spread.	More of a problem on spinach beet than beetroot.
See pages 18–19.	See pages 18–19.	
See pages 26–27.	See pages 26–27.	
See page 34.	See page 34.	
Choose varieties which are bolt resistant. Sow later.	Nothing can be done.	
See page 32.	See page 32.	
See pages 26–27.	See pages 26–27.	

Halo blight on French beans

Powdery mildew on peas

Pea leaf and pod spot

	TYPICAL SYMPTOMS	CAUSE	DETAILS
Cabbage Family Brassicas 	Plants grow poorly; may wilt and/or show red and purple tinges. Roots swollen and deformed.	**Club root** *Plasmodiophora brassicae* Fungal disease	This soil-living fungus can survive for 20 years in the absence of a suitable crop. Spread in soil and on infected plants.
	Chalky-white, blister-like pustules on leaves, which may look paint splashed.	**White blister** *Albugo candida* Fungal disease	A very distinctive disease which can infect all members of the cabbage family, also related ornamentals. A severe infection can reduce yields.
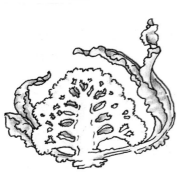	Yellowish spots or patches on upper surface of leaves; off-white mould below in damp weather.	**Downy mildew** *Peronospora parasitica* Fungal disease	Common on seedlings, which may be killed.
	Leaves and/or other parts with a white powdery coating. Infected leaves may drop.	**Crucifer powdery mildew** *Erysiphe cruciferarum* Fungal disease	A particular problem of swedes and turnips.
	Stunting, mosaics, ring spot and crinkling of leaves.	**Various mosaic viruses**	Cabbage family plants may get a range of viruses, often in combination. See pages 26–27.
	Leaves bluish green, often with brown scorched edges, oldest first. Growth poor.	**Potassium deficiency**	See page 35.
	Leaves with yellow, red or purplish tints, oldest first. Poor growth; no root damage.	**Nitrogen deficiency**	See pages 34–35.
	Brussels sprout buttons show browning inside when cut.	**Calcium deficiency**	See pages 32–33.
	Cauliflower curds show brownish patches when cut; also in stem.	**Boron deficiency**	See page 32.
	CHINESE CABBAGE Plants run to seed prematurely.	**Bolting** Disorder	Chinese cabbage is a 'short day' plant. The lengthening days of spring and early summer will encourage bolting.
	SPRING CABBAGE Plants run to seed prematurely.	**Bolting** Disorder	Plants that are too large when the winter cold comes will tend to bolt.
Carrots and Parsnips	Older leaves yellow from the edges; also red tints. New growth green.	**Magnesium deficiency**	See page 33.
	Purpling of older leaves in young crop, beginning at leaf edges. No root damage.	**Phosphorus deficiency**	See page 35.
	Leaves pale, appear frail. Older leaves yellow.	**Nitrogen deficiency**	See pages 34–35.

PREVENTION	ONCE INFECTED	REMARKS
Do not bring infected soil or plants into the garden. Lime soil before growing susceptible crops if soil is acid. Use a long rotation.	Dig up infected plants; do not add them to the compost heap. Raise plants in pots, then plant out into a hole filled with clean soil or compost. Grow kale, sprouting broccoli or cabbage which may produce a crop despite infection.	A most serious disease of the brassica family. Also infects wallflowers, mustard, stocks, radishes, swedes and turnips. One variety of swede has some resistance.

Club root on brassica

Crop rotation.	Remove infected plants and compost well. Severe attack may sometimes be limited by spraying with Bordeaux mixture, see page 61.	
See pages 18–19.	See pages 18–19.	
See pages 19–20.	See pages 19–20.	Also attacks wallflowers, related ornamentals and poppies.
Control of aphids and flea beetle can help to limit infection.	See pages 26–27.	
See page 35.	See page 35.	
See pages 34–35.	See pages 34–35.	
See pages 32–33.	See pages 32–33.	
See page 32.	See page 32.	

Turnip mosaic virus on brassica

Sow early summer on – or follow directions on packet.	
Do not sow too early.	

White blister on cabbage

See page 33.	See page 33.
See page 35.	See page 35.
See pages 34–35.	See pages 34–35.

TYPICAL SYMPTOMS	CAUSE	DETAILS

Carrots and Parsnips continued

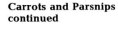

TYPICAL SYMPTOMS	CAUSE	DETAILS
Roots covered with a network of purple strands to which soil sticks.	**Violet root rot** *Helicobasidium brebissonii* Fungal disease	See page 21.
Roots split.	**Variable water supply** Disorder	Roots will tend to split if water is supplied after a very dry period.
CARROTS ONLY Leaves red, with fine yellow mottle; leaf stalks twist; plant stunted.	**Carrot motley dwarf** Viral disease	Caused by two viruses.

Celery and Celeriac

Leaves show small brown spots on which black pinheads develop, oldest leaves first.	**Celery leaf spot** *Septoria apicola* Fungal disease	Can spread quickly in damp weather. Seed and crop debris are main source of infection.
Leaf stalks rot at base; white cottony mould present.	**Sclerotinia** *Sclerotinia sclerotiorum* Fungal disease	See pages 20–21.
Leaves with pale spots, white mould beneath in damp weather.	**Downy mildew** *Peronospora nivea* Fungal disease	Also infects parsnips.
Leaves yellowed in various patterns. No pest present in leaves.	**Cucumber mosaic** and others Viral disease	See under cucurbits; also pages 26–27.
Leaves yellowed; leaf stalks discoloured and split. No root damage.	**Boron deficiency**	See page 32.
Plants run to flower prematurely.	**Bolting** Disorder	A check to growth caused by temperature below 12°C, or a shortage of water, can induce bolting.
Roots rotting, covered with dark purple strands.	**Violet root rot** *Helicobasidium brebissonii* Fungal disease	See page 21.

Cucurbits

Leaves with yellow mottling, may be crinkled or stunted. Fruits puckered, deformed.	**Cucumber mosaic** Viral disease	Dahlias, delphiniums and primulas can be a particular source of infection.
No fruit setting.	**Poor pollination** Disorder	Cold weather can curtail the action of pollinating insects. A shortage of water can also inhibit fruit set.
Leaves wilt, oldest first; brown discolouration in cut stem.	**Wilt** Various fungi Fungal disease	See page 22.
Leaves wilt in absence of other symptoms.	**Lack of water** Disorder	See pages 4–7.
Powdery white coating on leaves, in patches or overall.	**Powdery mildew** *Erysiphe cichoracearum, Sphaerotheca fuliginea* Fungal disease	These mildew-causing fungi occur on a wide range of plants.

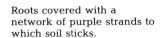

PREVENTION	ONCE INFECTED	REMARKS

See page 21.   See page 21.

Improve water holding of soil, see pages 5–6.   Nothing can be done.

Control of aphids may help limit spread. See also pages 26–27.   See pages 26–27.

Do not use seed from infected plants. Use a crop rotation.   Do not water infected plants from above. Remove infected plants and compost well.

See pages 20–21.   See pages 20–21.

See pages 18–19.   See pages 18–19.

Violet root rot on carrot

Aphid control and crop rotation can help to keep celery virus-free.   See pages 26–27.

See page 32.   See page 32.

Do not plant out or harden off plants too early. Improve water holding of soil, see pages 5–6.   Nothing can be done.

See page 21.   See page 21.

Scrupulous aphid control may limit it. Grow resistant varieties. See also pages 9, 26–27.   See pages 26–27.   Can infect over 700 plant species!

Powdery mildew on marrow

Keep plants adequately watered. Hand pollinate flowers.

See page 22.   See page 22.

Improve water-holding capacity of soil.   Water plants.

See pages 19–20.   See pages 19–20.   Often appears late in the season causing little damage.

TYPICAL SYMPTOMS	CAUSE	DETAILS
Cucurbits continued		
Plants grow poorly; roots decayed.	**Foot and root rots** Various fungi Fungal disease	See page 20.
Plants wilt; stem rotted at base where cottony mould may be seen.	**Sclerotinia** *Sclerotinia sclerotiorum* Fungal disease	See pages 20–21.
No fruit forming.	**Various causes** Disorder	Outdoor cucumbers, courgettes, etc., must be pollinated to set fruit.
Lettuce		
Plants wilt; red-brown rot at stem level. Fluffy grey mould may be present.	**Grey mould** *Botrytis cinerea* Fungal disease	Common in damp, cool weather, especially on plants already damaged or under stress. Survives on dead and dying plants.
Heads rot; stems may rot completely.	**Foot and root rots** Fungal disease	See page 20.
Plants wilt suddenly; stems rot at base where white cottony mould may be seen.	**Sclerotinia** *Sclerotinia sclerotiorum* Fungal disease	See pages 20–21.
Yellow patches on upper leaf surface, white mould beneath in damp weather. Patches turn brown and angular as leaf tissue dies.	**Downy mildew** *Bremia lactucae* Fungal disease	Seedlings and mature plants may suffer. Mildew weakens plants, paving the way for grey mould to move in.
Outer leaves with slight to intense yellowing between veins. Summer crops.	**Beet western yellows** Viral disease	Spread by aphids. Also affects endive, beet and spinach.
Leaves have a marbled look, pale between the veins. Plants stunted.	**Lettuce mosaic** Viral disease	Symptoms appear in early spring. Seed-borne and aphid spread.
Outer leaves distorted and blistered, usually on older plants.	**Lettuce big vein** Viral disease	Virus lives in the soil and is passed on by a fungus. It can survive for 15 years.
Leaves pale; growth poor; small heart.	**Nitrogen deficiency**	See pages 34–35.
Older leaves with severe scorching round edges and between veins.	**Potassium deficiency**	See page 35.
Leaves scorched round edges.	**Calcium deficiency** (Tipburn)	See pages 32–33.
Growth severely reduced; plants fail to heart. No other symptoms.	**Phosphorus deficiency**	See page 35.
Onions, Chives, Leeks, Garlic and Shallots		
Bright orange pustules on leaves – especially on leeks and chives – in summer and in autumn.	**Leek rust** *Puccinia allii* Fungal disease	A severe infection may kill young plants but otherwise the disease does not usually affect yield of crop.

PREVENTION	ONCE INFECTED	REMARKS
See page 20.	See page 20.	
See pages 20–21.	See pages 20–21.	
See pages 28–30.		
Good growing and hygiene. Do not water lettuce plants from above.	Remove infected plants and dispose of in a hot compost heap or outside the garden.	Found on a wide range of plants.
See page 20.	See page 20.	
See pages 20–21.	See pages 20–21.	
See pages 18–19.	See pages 18–19.	
Strict aphid control. Clean up crop debris. Cos and crisp varieties are more tolerant than others.	See pages 26–27.	
Grow resistant varieties. See also pages 9, 26–27.	See pages 26–27.	
Where it is endemic, raise plants in large pots before planting out. See also pages 26–27.	See pages 26–27.	
See pages 34–35.	See pages 34–35.	
See page 35.	See page 35.	
See pages 32–33.	See pages 32–33.	
See page 35.	See page 35.	
Do not overfeed with nitrogen. Correct potash shortages. Correct any drainage problem. Break the cycle.	Wait! The disease often disappears of its own accord in the autumn.	Often looks worse than it is.

Calcium deficiency in lettuce

Rust on leek

	TYPICAL SYMPTOMS	CAUSE	DETAILS
Onions, Chives, Leeks, Garlic and Shallots continued	Leaves die back; roots poor; fluffy white mould on base of bulb. Mould may contain black, pinhead-sized fungal resting bodies.	**White rot** *Sclerotium cepivorum* Fungal disease	Young plants may die; older ones crop poorly. White rot resting bodies survive 15 or more years in the soil in absence of a crop. Disease spread in soil and on infected plants.
	Leaves yellow and die from tip down. Off-white to purplish mould grows on dead leaves in damp weather.	**Downy mildew** *Peronospora destructor* Fungal disease	Bulbs may also rot in store. See pages 18–19.
	Leaves die back from tip, without becoming yellow.	**Potassium deficiency**	See page 35.
	Onions, shallots and garlic which have been in store for at least 10 weeks show a soft rot which starts in the neck. A fluffy grey mould may also be present.	**Onion neck rot** *Botrytis aclada* Fungal disease	Infected seed, plants and crop debris are main sources of infection.
	OVERWINTERING ONIONS Plants run to seed prematurely.	**Bolting** Disorder	Overwintering varieties will bolt if plants are too large when the winter cold comes.
Parsnips	Small brown spots on leaves; orange-brown roughening of skin on shoulder of roots; small dark lesions on roots.	**Parsnip canker** Various fungi Fungal disease	Three different organisms can be involved in causing parsnip canker.
Peas (see Beans and Peas)			
Potatoes	Brown blotches on leaves, with white mould underneath in damp weather. Foliage rapidly destroyed in warm, humid weather. Infected tubers may rot in store.	**Potato blight** *Phytophthora infestans* Fungal disease	Seed tubers, 'volunteer' plants left to grow from an infected crop, and ornamental *Solanaceae* are the main source of infection. Symptoms first appear May/June.
	Brown patches appear overnight on upper foliage, early in the season.	**Frost** Disorder	See pages 9–10, 28–30.
	Upward rolling of lower leaves a few weeks after emergence. Spreads to upper leaves which go stiff/brittle.	**Potato leaf roll** Viral disease	Symptoms of potato viruses may not show up, particularly in the first year of infection.
	Plants stunted, leaves puckered and mottled. Tubers few and small.	**Potato virus Y**	As for potato leaf roll.
	Leaves yellow between veins, lowest first.	**Manganese deficiency**	See page 34.
	Leaves small and pale. Growth poor, few tubers.	**Nitrogen deficiency**	See pages 34–35.

PREVENTION	ONCE INFECTED	REMARKS
Do not bring in soil or plants that may be contaminated. Raise plants in modules. Plant out at 15 cm or wider spacing. See pages 18–19.	Dig up infected plants along with a large scoop of soil and dispose of it outside the garden. See pages 18–19.	A major problem of onions and garlic; less so on leeks.

White rot on stored onion

See page 35.	See page 35.	
Clear up crop debris. Crop rotation (minimum 3 years). Wide spacing. Do not overfeed plants with nitrogen. Avoid damage to plants; do not bend onion leaves over.	Nothing can be done.	Infection starts in young plants, but symptoms do not show up until crops are in store. Dry onions well before storing.

Timing of sowing is critical. Southern areas – last week August; Midlands – mid-August; North – first week August.	Nothing can be done.	

Neck rot on onion

Grow resistant varieties. Grow on well-drained site. Crop rotation. Grow at 7.5 to 10 cm spacing; small parsnips are less prone.	Nothing can be done.	
Buy new seed tubers each year. Grow less susceptible varieties, e.g. Wilja, Cara. Where blight is a regular problem, grow early varieties which will produce a decent yield before the disease appears.	Cut off all foliage to ground level; remove it to the compost heap. Then wait 3 weeks before digging up the crop. This will help reduce spread to tubers. Bordeaux mixture may slow down spread if applied early enough, see page 61.	

Potato blight

See pages 9–10, 28–30.	See pages 9–10, 28–30.	
Buy certified virus-free planting tubers. See also pages 9, 26–27.	Tubers saved from an infected crop will show greater symptoms in following years and cropping will decline.	
As for potato leaf roll. See also pages 9, 26–27.		
See page 34.	See page 34.	
See pages 34–35.	See pages 34–35.	

	TYPICAL SYMPTOMS	CAUSE	DETAILS
Potatoes continued	Leaves yellow between veins, usually with a green band round edges.	**Magnesium deficiency**	See page 33.
	Leaves scorched at edges and may curl, oldest first. Poor crop.	**Potassium deficiency**	See page 35.
	Individual stems or plants grow poorly; leaves roll. The base of infected stems turn dark brown for 10 cm above and below ground. In wet weather, stem base and tubers rot to smelly mass.	**Blackleg** *Erwinia carotovora* Bacterial disease	Seed tubers are main source of infection. There is little spread between plants except in wet soils. Tubers may rot in store.
	Stems rot at base; white cottony mould present.	**Sclerotinia** *Sclerotinia sclerotiorum* Fungal disease	See pages 20–21.
	Tubers have rounded corky, scabby patches on surface. Little effect on crop.	**Common scab** *Streptomyces scabies* Bacterial disease	The scab bacteria is common in most soils, but the disease shows up mainly in light soils and in those with a high pH. Most common in dry seasons.
	Tubers have irregular, brown, crater-like depressions with raised, ragged edges. Sometimes develop canker-like growths.	**Powdery scab** *Spongospora subterranea* Fungal disease	A soil-living disease which is most common in heavy soils and in wet seasons. It can survive 10 years or more in the absence of a suitable crop.
Spinach	Plants run to seed prematurely.	**Bolting** Disorder	Day lengths of 13 hours or more will prompt spinach to bolt.
	Pale yellow patches on leaves, greyish mould beneath in damp weather.	**Downy mildew** *Peronospora farinosa* Fungal disease	See pages 18–19.
Tomatoes	Leaves with dark blotches, may have white mould growth underneath. Fruit with tough, dryish brown rot which may not develop until after picking.	**Potato blight** *Phytophthora infestans* Fungal disease	Spreads from potato crops. See potato blight, pages 46–47.
	Foliage discolours; plants wilt. Roots and/or base of stem rots.	**Foot and root rots** Fungal disease	See page 20.
	Leaves wilt, oldest first. May recover at night. Brown streaks in cut stem well above soil level.	**Wilt** Various fungi Fungal disease	See page 22.
	Fruit has tough dark patch where blossom was attached.	**Calcium deficiency** (Blossom end rot)	See pages 32–33.
	Fruits split.	**Splitting** Disorder	See pages 28–30.

PREVENTION	ONCE INFECTED	REMARKS
See page 33.	See page 33.	
See page 35.	See page 35.	
Grow less susceptible varieties, e.g. Ailsa, Wilja, Maris Piper. Avoid poorly drained site. Crop rotation. Good hygiene. Do not mulch early.	Dispose of infected plants in a good compost heap or outside the garden. Harvest every tuber.	Most common where soil is cool and wet soon after planting.
See pages 20–21.	See pages 20–21.	

Common scab on potato

Grow resistant varieties, e.g. Wilja, Pentland Javelin. Do not lime soil before growing potatoes. Add lawn mowings to planting trench to make soil more acid. Buy certified virus-free planting tubers.	Nothing can be done.	Most common in dry seasons; the best time to reduce scab is when the plants meet between the rows. Foliage from infected crops can be composted.
Avoid wet soils.	Use as long a rotation as possible. Do not compost scabbed peelings.	
Grow spinach in the short days of autumn, winter and spring.		
See pages 18–19.	See pages 18–19.	
	Bordeaux mixture, see page 61.	
See page 20.	See page 20.	
See page 22.	See page 22.	
See pages 32–33.	See pages 32–33.	
See pages 28–30.	See pages 28–30.	

Calcium deficiency in tomato

TYPICAL SYMPTOMS	CAUSE	DETAILS

All Fruit
Applies to all fruit in this chart unless indicated

TYPICAL SYMPTOMS	CAUSE	DETAILS
Blossom wilts and may not set. Flowers and young emerging canes brown and die suddenly. Young leaves 'scorched'. Poor cropping.	**Frost** Disorder	See pages 9–10, 28–30.
Growth and cropping poor; leaves with irregular colouring effects.	**Virus**	See pages 26–27.
Black sticky mould covers leaves and fruit.	**Sooty mould** *Cladosporium* spp. and others Fungal disease	See pages 16–17, 24.
Flowers: death of flowers revealed by poor crop (particularly blackcurrants), not apparent until later in season. *Fruits*: become rotten; grey fluffy mould spreads over rotted area. *Branches*: may die back with no other symptoms (currants and gooseberries).	**Grey mould** *Botrytis cinerea* Fungal disease	See pages 16–17, 23.
Creeping death across patch of garden or trees/bushes dying in succession. Branches die back; bark near base of stem pulls away, revealing white sheets smelling of mushrooms.	**Honey fungus** *Armillaria mellea* Fungal disease	See pages 16–17, 23–24.

Apples and Pears

TYPICAL SYMPTOMS	CAUSE	DETAILS
Blossom and young shoots wilt. Leaves turn brown (black in pears) but hang on tree limply. Shoots ooze slime.	**Fireblight** *Erwinia amylovora* Bacterial disease	Trees give appearance of 'scorching' by fire. Progression of disease much more rapid in pears. Wood under bark near affected areas may show mottled or red-brown colouring. Worst in warm, wet summers.
Blossom wilts; fruit spurs die during or after flowering. Fruits with soft brown patches; concentric rings of white spots.	**Brown rot** *Sclerotinia fructigena* and *Sclerotinia laxa* Fungal disease	Dehydrated fruits hang in tree over winter. See plums, pages 56–57.
Strange leaf tints; poor growth generally; fruit possibly highly coloured.	**Nitrogen, phosphorus or potassium deficiency**	See pages 34–35.
Leaves and fruit bruised, or leaves tattered, or fruits marked.	**Wind or hail damage** Disorder	See pages 10, 30.
Leaves and flowers covered in white powdery coating; in winter, branch tips are distorted and slightly discoloured.	**Powdery mildew** *Podosphaera leucotricha* Fungal disease	First infection from overwintered spores or buds to new leaves and blossoms. These become white and powdery then eventually drop. Without treatment, the disease spreads progressively.
Leaves brown with silvery sheen; some branches may die back.	**Silver leaf** *Chondrostereum purpureum* Fungal disease	See plums, pages 58–59.

PREVENTION	ONCE INFECTED	REMARKS
See pages 7, 9–10.	See pages 9–10, 28–30.	See also brown rot and fireblight, under individual fruit entries.
See pages 26–27.	See pages 26–27.	See also mineral deficiences, pages 31–35.
See pages 16–17, 24.	See pages 16–17, 24.	
See pages 16–17, 23.	See pages 16–17, 23.	Mainly a problem of soft fruit. Can affect stored apples and pears.
See pages 16–17, 23–24.	See pages 16–17, 23–24.	Fruits in this chart not affected: strawberries.
If fireblight is known in your area, then avoid planting susceptible ornamentals (see remarks) or hawthorn hedges. Inspect trees regularly.	Immediate severe pruning to at least 45cm beyond the affected area may save the tree. Severely infected plants must be dug out and burnt.	Also affects ornamental plants of the rose family (*Rosaceae*): Pyracantha, Crataegus, Cotoneaster, Sorbus, Amelanchier, Chaenomeles, Stranvaesia. See also frost, brown rot.
Handle apples and pears for storage gently to avoid bruising.		Different strains of the fungus exist and brown rot on plums is unlikely to pass to apples or pears.
See pages 34–35.	See pages 34–35.	Fruit tastes very sweet or unpleasant.
See pages 10, 30.	See pages 10, 30.	Windbreaks may limit damage, see page 7.
Choose resistant varieties. Do not let trees suffer drought stress. Inspect trees regularly.	Pick off earliest infected leaves. Take care not to shake spores onto healthy leaves. Prune out mildewed shoots to healthy wood.	Unusual on pears but common on apples, especially in dry seasons. Regular and persistent attacks can be sprayed with sulphur, see page 61.
See pages 58–59.	See pages 58–59.	Mainly affects plums. Can also affect apples, cherries, currants and gooseberries.

Frost damage on raspberry

Grey mould on strawberry

Powdery mildew on apple

51

	TYPICAL SYMPTOMS	CAUSE	DETAILS

Apples and Pears continued

	TYPICAL SYMPTOMS	CAUSE	DETAILS
	Leaves with olive/green blotches, becoming black. May fall early with yellowish colouration. Fruits covered in black spots, sometimes cracked or corky.	**Scab** *Venturia inaequalis* and *Venturia pirina* Fungal disease	Apple scab and pear scab are similar in symptoms but are distinct fungal species. Common and unsightly but not disastrous as fruits are still edible. First leaf symptoms appear late spring onwards and then infect developing fruits. In a bad attack fruits are cracked quite deeply and leaves fall prematurely. Pears are distorted.
	Leaves with yellow marbling between veins.	**Magnesium deficiency**	See page 33.
	Leaves thick and narrow, develop 'rosettes'; some die-back of branches. Fruit cracked or split.	**Boron deficiency**	See page 32.
	Pink pustules on dead material.	**Coral spot** *Nectria cinnabarina* Fungal disease	See page 22.
	Cracks round base of shoots or on branches; wrinkled, discoloured and sunken areas of bark; death of spur, shoot or branch.	**Canker** *Nectria galligena* Fungal disease	Infects through cracks in bark or buds, pruning cuts or any fresh wound, including scars where leaves detach. Canker may completely girdle a branch in which case it dies beyond the wound. Sometimes spurs and twigs die from canker with no other symptoms.
	Fruits cracked or split; splitting of bark; no other symptoms.	**Drought followed by heavy rain** Disorder	See pages 4–7, 28–30.
	Fruit skins pitted; dark spots in flesh; fruit tastes bitter.	**Bitter pit** (drought-induced calcium shortage) Disorder/deficiency	Symptoms in fruit caused by failure in calcium supply, but real cause nearly always dry soil preventing movement of calcium.
	Excessively vigorous growth; poor fruiting.	**Overfeeding** Disorder **Bad planting** Disorder	See pages 13, 30. See page 12.
	Stored fruit rots.	**Storage rots** *Penicillium* spp. and others Fungal/bacterial disease	See page 24.

Blackberries, Hybrid Berries and Raspberries

	Purple spots on canes, leaves and blossom stalks, becoming white and sunken later in summer. Loganberry fruits develop one-sided.	**Cane spot** *Elsinoe veneta* Fungal disease	Infection passes from fruiting canes to new canes in May and June. Further infections develop from these in late summer. Severe infections cause premature leaf fall, distortion and even death of canes.

PREVENTION	ONCE INFECTED	REMARKS
Plant resistant varieties. Rake up autumn leaves and remove from site, or use rotary mower over leaves to speed decomposition. Spraying leaves with urine, liquid manure or other high nitrogen material also speeds rotting. Keep habit of tree open by pruning.	Prune out affected twigs in winter and burn. Spraying with sulphur will limit spread but is not advisable, see page 61.	Affected fruits can be stored but other rotting diseases may enter through the scab lesions. Disease most prevalent in sultry, humid and damp summers. For detailed cycle of how scab spreads, see page 17.
See page 33.	See page 33.	
See page 32.	See page 32.	Fruit symptoms similar to those caused by scab and drought followed by heavy rain.
Prune carefully and burn infected branches.	See page 22.	Very common on pea-sticks.
Choose less susceptible varieties. Do not overfeed trees. Do not plant trees on badly drained sites. Attend to soil structure before planting.	Inspect trees regularly and prune out any canker as soon as seen. Burn diseased material and cover wound with suitable sealant.	Fruit may be affected: brown rot round the eye, fruit hangs in tree all winter. Most common on old trees and where roots are restricted or drainage is poor.
See pages 4–7, 28–30.	See pages 4–7, 28–30.	See also scab and boron deficiency.
Ensure plenty of water in dry conditions. Mulch well. Severe summer pruning of young growth can reduce bitter pit.	Nothing can be done in that year.	'Bramley's seedling' apple is particularly prone. Do not overfeed, see pages 13, 30. Not a problem every year!
See pages 13, 30.	See pages 13, 30.	
See page 12.	See page 12.	
See page 24.		
Avoid use of susceptible varieties. Plant new canes well away from infected plants.	Prune out affected canes and burn them. If attack has become severe, then spray with Bordeaux mixture, see page 61, fortnightly from budburst to petal fall.	Blackberry cane spot (*Septoria rubi*) and purple blotch (*Septocyta ramealis*) are similar diseases affecting blackberries only. Not usually serious.

Scab on apple

Canker on apple

Bitter pit on apple

Cane spot on raspberry

	TYPICAL SYMPTOMS	CAUSE	DETAILS
Blackberries, Hybrid Berries and Raspberries continued 	Canes fail to leaf in spring or start growth and wither; canes pull away from soil easily; often, overwintered canes are brittle and dead.	**Cane blight** *Leptosphaeria coniothyrium* Fungal disease	Disease enters from soil, usually through wounds caused by wind damage, feeding of cane midges, etc. Spreads easily from infected canes or movement of contaminated soil in the garden.
	Purple stained patches on canes usually centred round a developing bud/leaf axil. Turns silvery in winter and covered in tiny black dots.	**Spur blight** *Didymella applanata* Fungal disease	Very common debilitating disease but not a killer. Common in wet springs. In very hot summers may cause shrivelling of fruits. Wind spreads infection from black dots (conidia) of winter stage to new canes in spring. Buds within a patch of infection may fail to grow.
	Canes with hard irregular swellings. Similar swellings possible on roots.	**Crown gall** *Agrobacterium tumefaciens* Bacterial disease	Swellings not consistent in size or shape. Eventually break to release bacteria for further infections. Not usually serious.
	Canes die progressively; roots killed but not decayed.	**Phytophthora root disease** *Phytophthora* spp. Fungal disease	Serious disease typical of wet or waterlogged soils. Spores swim in soil water to infect roots which are quickly killed but do not rot.
	Leaves covered in white powdery coating; flowers possibly distorted; fruit inedible.	**Powdery mildew** *Sphaerotheca macularis* Fungal disease	See strawberries, pages 58–59, and pages 19–20.
	Leaves wilt suddenly; blue stripe on one side of cane.	**Blue stripe wilt** *Verticillium* spp. Fungal disease	Soil-borne disease. Effects visible any time in spring or summer, especially in hot weather. Wilting is sudden and blue striping gives final clue. Canes die. Disease will spread through row.
Blackcurrants, Redcurrants and Whitecurrants 	White powdery coating on leaves and young shoots. Shoots may die back.	**American gooseberry mildew** *Sphaerotheca mors-uvae* Fungal disease	See gooseberries, pages 56–57.
	Poor cropping	**Mineral deficiency** **Water shortage** Disorder	See pages 31–35. See pages 4–7.
	Small brown spots on leaves in June; leaves eventually yellow and fall early.	**Leaf spot** *Pseudopeziza ribis* Fungal disease	Spreads by wind and fallen leaves. New leaves show spotting by mid-June. Spots may coalesce. Leaves yellow and drop prematurely, under-sides glisten in wet weather.
	Branches and roots with knobbly or warty irregular growths and swellings.	**Grown gall** *Agrobacterium tumefaciens* Bacterial disease	See blackberries, pages 54–55.
	Branches die back; leaves silvered.	**Silver leaf** *Chondrostereum purpureum* Fungal disease	See plums, pages 58–59.

PREVENTION	ONCE INFECTED	REMARKS

Control cane midges if known to be a problem (see Organic Handbook 2). Prevent wind damage by supporting growing canes well. Obtain new raspberry plants from a reputable source.

Cut out canes below soil level as soon as diagnosed and burn them. Disinfect secateurs afterwards.

More common on raspberries than blackberries, but may cause a root rot on strawberries. Plant new canes well away from infected plants. Do not propagate from known infected stock.

Spur blight on loganberry

Some varieties less susceptible. Thin canes early in the season to approximately 10–15 per m. Regularly remove unwanted canes during the season.

Prune out and burn affected canes. If spur blight is a regular problem, then spray with Bordeaux mixture, see page 61, when canes are about 10cm tall, and three times more at fortnightly intervals.

Do not plant fruit in soil from which previously infected plants have been removed.

Prune out and burn infected canes, roots or stems before galls burst.

Can also affect currants, cherries, and many woody and herbaceous ornamental plants.

Avoid unsuitable soils and sites.

Dig up and burn affected canes. Disinfect tools. Grass over site and do not replant.

Can also affect apples as well as many other ornamental plants. Common in Scotland.

See pages 19–20, 58–59.

See pages 19–20, 58–59.

None possible, but disinfect tools which have been used on infected plants.

Dig out whole plant with as much soil as possible and destroy. If disease persists, then grub out row and replant new healthy canes elsewhere. Wait 6 years before reusing site.

Also affects strawberries and many ornamentals, but not blackberries or hybrid berries. Blue striping is unique to raspberries. Not common.

Cane blight on raspberry

See pages 56–57.

See pages 56–57.

Not common on red or whitecurrants.

See pages 31–35.
See pages 4–7.

See pages 31–35.
See pages 4–7.

Avoid susceptible varieties such as Baldwin. Prune out drooping growth close to soil.

Clear away and burn all fallen leaves. Pick off newly infected leaves and destroy. After harvest, spray with Bordeaux mixture, page 61.

Not common on blackcurrants. Also affects gooseberries. Severe attacks can progressively defoliate and weaken bushes.

See pages 54–55.

See pages 54–55.

See pages 58–59.

See pages 58–59.

Mainly affects plums.

Gooseberries, Worcesterberries and Jostaberries

TYPICAL SYMPTOMS	CAUSE	DETAILS
Leaves, shoot tips, spurs and fruits covered with white powdery coating.	**American gooseberry mildew** *Sphaerotheca mors-uvae* Fungal disease	Particularly troublesome in very humid summers when soil is dry. Infection spread on the wind or from overwintered spores on buds and fallen leaves. First sign is white powdery coating on young leaves from June onwards. Spreads to affect all young growth and fruit. Coating thickens, becomes brown and felty: growth is distorted and may die back.
Leaves covered in brown spots or patches from mid-June; leaves yellow and fall early.	**Leaf spot** *Pseudopeziza ribis* Fungal disease	See blackcurrants, pages 54–55.
Leaves yellow between veins.	**Manganese deficiency**	See page 34.
Branches die back; leaves silvered.	**Silver leaf** *Chondrostereum purpureum* Fungal disease	See plums, pages 58–59.
Branches die back; pink pustules on dead wood.	**Coral spot** *Nectria cinnabarina* Fungal disease	See page 22.
Branches and possibly roots with irregular, hard, knobbly swellings.	**Crown gall** *Agrobacterium tumefaciens* Bacterial disease	See blackberries, pages 54–55.
Fruits split.	**Drought followed by heavy rain** Disorder	See pages 4–7, 28–30.

Plums, Damsons and Cherries

TYPICAL SYMPTOMS	CAUSE	DETAILS
Blossom wilts; fruit spurs or terminal shoots die; fruit with soft rotten patches, developing concentric rings of white pustules.	**Brown rot** *Sclerotinia fructigena* and *Sclerotinia laxa* Fungal disease	*Sclerotinia laxa* enters blossoms and leaves, and forms a canker in fruit spurs and twiggy growth which then dies. Blossom wilts but remains on tree. *Sclerotinia fructigena* spreads through fruit. The fungus enters through wounds caused by weather, insects or birds, and causes soft brown rot which spreads to other fruit by contact. Concentric rings of white pustules grow on soft patches, and spores from these spread the infection.
Leaves with many holes as if blasted with shot; soft depressions in bark, sometimes oozing gum; branches may die back.	**Bacterial canker** *Pseudomonas mors-prunorum* Bacterial disease	Leaf symptoms appear in late spring as small brown spots which later drop out to leave 'shot hole' appearance. Bacteria splashed from these leaves in autumn start new infections on stems. These create shallow depressions which may exude gum (especially cherries). These lesions expand in spring, often on one side of branch only. Affected areas feel squashy and look flattened. If branch is girdled, then growth beyond the canker dies. Lesions frequently heal and are not necessarily progressive but new infections pass to leaves in spring.

PREVENTION	ONCE INFECTED	REMARKS

Allow proper spacing between plants and keep an open framework by summer and winter pruning. Keep bushes weed-free, mulched and well watered in dry conditions. Do not overfeed bushes. Choose resistant varieties.

Prune out all infections and distorted tips. If mildew persists, then spray from first signs with bicarbonate of soda, see page 61, weekly until September.

Fruit is still edible if mould is wiped away. Also affects currants, especially blackcurrants.

American gooseberry mildew

See pages 54–55.

See pages 54–55.

See page 34.

See page 34.

See pages 58–59.

See pages 58–59.

See page 22.

See page 22.

See pages 54–55.

See pages 54–55.

Also affects cane fruits.

See pages 4–7, 28–30.

See pages 4–7, 28–30.

Maintain good garden hygiene. Thin fruit early to prevent bruising and keep birds away if possible.

Prune out all wilted blossom spurs and affected twigs; remove mummified fruit. Paint all pruning cuts with *Trichoderma viride* paste, see page 61.

Also affects apples and pears. Fruit dehydrates and hangs 'mummified' in tree over winter.

Coral spot

Avoid susceptible varieties, e.g. Victoria. Take care when staking and tying in not to wound tree. Plums grafted on to Myrobalan rootstock and cherries on F12/1 (Mazzard) have some resistance. (These rootstocks are very vigorous and produce large trees).

Prune all cankered limbs back to healthy wood as soon as possible and burn infected branches. Paint all cuts with *Trichoderma* paste, see page 61. If disease becomes persistent, then spray with Bordeaux mixture in mid-August, mid-September and mid-October. Note that Bordeaux mixture can cause early leaf fall, see page 61.

Gumming on stems or fruit does not necessarily indicate bacterial canker. May be result of drought stress, wounding or, possibly, virus.

Bacterial canker on Victoria plum

	TYPICAL SYMPTOMS	CAUSE	DETAILS
Plums, Damsons and Cherries continued 	Leaves with bright yellow spots from July, becoming black; leaves yellow and fall early.	**Plum rust** *Tranzschelia pruni-spinosae* Fungal disease	Wind-borne disease. Bright yellow spots on upper surface of leaf with corresponding brown powdery patch underneath. Spots turn black by autumn, leaves yellow and fall early. New infections from fallen leaves and on wind.
	Leaves become silvered progressively; brown stain in wood; branches die back.	**Silver leaf** *Chondrostereum purpureum* Fungal disease	Spores enter through wounds between September and May. Leaves become silvered, usually on one branch only at first and then progressively through tree. Affected branches reveal dark brown discolouration in wood. Die back. In summer, lilac coloured bracket fungi grow on dead branches to spread the disease.
	Stems and roots with hard, knobbly, irregular swellings.	**Crown gall** *Agrobacterium tumefaciens* Bacterial disease	See blackberries, pages 54–55.
	Plums grow one-sided, twisted and elongated, no stone; white bloom covers fruit which falls.	**Pocket plums** *Taphrina pruni* Fungal disease	Infection passes from fruit to twig before fruit falls. Reinfection to new fruit in spring.
	Fruit splits; possible splits in bark.	**Drought followed by heavy rain** Disorder	See pages 4–7, 28–30.
Strawberries	Leaves with red blotches, grey powdery coating underneath; leaf margins curl upwards. Flowers distorted, fruit inedible.	**Powdery mildew** *Sphaerotheca macularis* Fungal disease	Spread from old leaves and on the wind. Especially common in hot, dry weather. Leaf symptoms may occur from spring onwards, progressing to distortion or failure of flowers and inedible fruits.
	Stunted plants, outer leaves brown, inner leaves small, reddish; roots decayed and black or brown.	**Red core** *Phytophthora fragariae* Fungal disease	Distinguishable in winter from other root rots by central core of root being red; outer tissue peels away easily. Usually appears in late spring to early summer. Serious and persistent soil-borne disease – can last 12 years or more without a host.
	Outer leaves wilt; black or brown streaking inside leaf stalks.	**Wilt** *Verticillium* spp. Fungal disease	Closely allied to Blue Stripe.
	Leaves very pale, yellow or purplish; poor general growth.	**Mineral deficiency** **Drought** Disorder	See pages 31–35. See pages 4–7, 28–30.

PREVENTION	ONCE INFECTED	REMARKS
As for apple scab, see pages 17, 52–53.		Control is difficult, but disease not usually serious.
Prune between early June and late August. Paint all pruning cuts with *Trichoderma viride*, see page 61. Avoid susceptible varieties, e.g. Victoria.	Prune back dead branches to healthy, unstained wood. Paint cuts with *Trichoderma* paste. Affected trees can recover completely if treated with *Trichoderma viride* pellets, page 61, in August or February/March of the following year.	Silvering of leaves simultaneously, without staining or branch death, is caused by nutritional disorder brought on by shortage of water or mineral deficiency. Also affects currants, gooseberries and apples.
See pages 54–55.	See pages 54–55.	
None possible.	Collect up all affected fruit from ground or tree and destroy. If disease is persistent, then spray with Bordeaux mixture, see page 61, before flower buds open.	Cherries not affected. Prevalent in Northern Europe but uncommon in Britain except in western and northern areas.
See pages 4–7, 28–30.	See pages 4–7, 28–30.	
Allow adequate space between plants. Water plants well in dry weather, preferably by drip or seep system rather than overhead (encourages grey mould, see page 23). Trim off all leaves, runners and fruit stalks after harvest.	Pick off affected leaves as soon as seen. Sulphur can be sprayed fortnightly from just before flowering, see page 61. Choose less susceptible varieties. In autumn, remove all compost, hay or straw used for mulching.	Also affects blackberries, raspberries and hybrid berries.
Always remove strawberry crowns after 3 years of cropping. Replant in new site with runners or potted crowns from a reputable source. Attend to drainage problems.	Nothing available to amateurs. Isolate infected land and avoid walking on it or cultivating it. Grass down plot, then sterilise all tools and boots to avoid cross-contamination.	Soil becomes contaminated by planting diseased runners or by passage of soil on tools or boots. In Britain, suspicion of this disease must be notified to the Ministry of Agriculture, Fisheries and Food.
See raspberries, pages 54–55.		
See pages 31–35. See pages 4–7, 28–30.	See pages 31–35. See pages 4–7, 28–30.	

Sprays and paints for disease control

Safer sprays?

Most of the sprays included here can be used in commercial organic production, according to the standards set by the Soil Association (SA) and the United Kingdom Register of Organic Food Standards (UKROFS). The Soil Association standards do, however, put them in a 'restricted' category, not for routine use. This is because they are not harmless. They may be less harmful or less persistent than many, but they are poisons and will, inevitably, harm creatures other than those we wish to kill. Some of the sprays included are not yet approved for use in the UK and, therefore, cannot be used in either organic or conventional growing systems.

Effective spraying

All sprays, whatever their nature, should be used correctly. This is essential both to ensure that they are effective, and also so that harm to the environment is minimised. The sprays listed here are best used to *prevent* a disease rather than to clear it up once it has occurred. It is only worth considering using one if you have a persistent, recurrent problem.

● **Dos**

Identify the problem first, then choose an appropriate spray.

Read the label and instructions carefully before opening the bottle.

Use a sprayer suitable for the job – one that is in good condition, gives a good even spray and does not leak.

Use the exact dilutions recommended and only make up the quantity of spray that you need.

Adjust the sprayer so that it gives good cover of the area being sprayed. Too coarse a spray will mean that a lot of the spray just runs off the plant; too fine a spray may result in the spray drifting on to other plants.

Spray in still weather to reduce spray drift.

Apply the spray to the relevant area. If a spray only works by direct contact with a disease, then there is no point in spraying parts of the plant that are not infected.

Store pesticides in their original packaging, in a secure, cool, dark place.

● **Don'ts**

Use a spray just because it is the only one you have at the time.

Use a spray against diseases other than those for which it is recommended.

Add a little bit extra 'just in case' when diluting a pesticide.

Store made-up pesticides.

Spray in windy weather.

Spray plants where bees are working.

Store pesticides in unmarked bottles and in places accessible to children.

Never spray a crop where bees are working. This means that when plants are in flower they should not be sprayed. If it is essential to spray, then only do so in the evening when the bees have finished working. Alternatively, spray on cool early mornings when the bees are less active.

If there are bee keepers in your neighbourhood, then give them advance warning of any spraying.

What to use

Bicarbonate of soda

A culinary raising agent, unexpectedly useful in the garden. How it works is uncertain. Appears both to kill fungus and prevent spores germinating. Therefore, used as a preventative and cure.

Use against
Powdery mildews.

When and where
As a *preventative* for gooseberry mildew on blackcurrants and gooseberries, from just before flowering, fortnightly, until the end of August. Use 5 g per litre of water, adding soft soap or other wetting agent at about 1% of the solution (i.e. 10 ml per litre). As a *cure* for powdery mildews as soon as first symptoms are seen, used at 10 g per litre of water. Spray every 7 to 10 days.

Caution
Appears to be harmless to insects, although the wetting agent may kill some beneficial predatory insects. Use not approved in the UK.

Bordeaux mixture

A mixture of copper sulphate and quicklime, used to prevent disease infection and spread.

Use against
Potato blight, diseases of raspberries and blackberries, bacterial canker of plums and cherries, canker of apples.

When and where
See under individual disease entries.

Caution
Copper is harmful to some plants and can cause defoliation if used incorrectly. Do not use on plants under stress. Regular use could lead to a build-up of copper in the soil to toxic levels. Harmful to fish.

Sulphur

Available as a made-up solution, as a wettable powder and as a dust. Used to prevent disease infection and spread.

Use against
Powdery mildews, apple scab.

When and where
See under individual disease entries. Unlikely to be effective if disease is already established in the crop.

Caution
Safe to humans and animals but poisonous to some beneficial creatures such as predatory mites and parasitic wasps. Do not use on young apples or gooseberries, on plants under stress, or on fruit to be bottled or frozen. Sulphur should not be used on 'sulphur-shy' varieties of fruit as it may harm them.

Some sulphur-shy gooseberry varieties: Careless, Leveller, Early Sulphur, Golden Drop, Lord Derby, Roaring Lion.

Some sulphur-shy apple varieties: Stirling Castle, St Cecilia, Beauty of Bath, Belle de Boskoop, Blenheim Orange, Cox's Orange Pippin, Duchess's Favourite, Lane's Prince Albert, Lord Derby, Newton Wonder, Rival.

If in doubt about a variety, then spray a few leaves only at first; check for damage after a day or two.

Trichoderma viride

Trichoderma is a fungus, harmless to plants, which has an antagonistic effect on some other fungi. It is available as a wettable powder, or in pellet form.

Use against
Silver leaf on cherries and plums; as a general preventative on pruning cuts.

When and where
Use *pellets* to protect cherries and plums from silver leaf infection; also to protect the healthy parts of lightly infected trees. They are applied to holes drilled in the tree, during February to April, or in August. The *wettable powder* is made up into a paste with seaweed extract, bentonite clay or soft soap and applied to pruning cuts within half an hour of cutting. Treat *all* cuts on plums and cherries; only larger wounds (over 2.5 cm across) need protection on apples and pears. *Trichoderma* is not approved for use in the UK at present.

Glossary

Bed system: a system of growing in which the garden is divided up into narrow beds which are separated by paths.

Biodegradable: able to be broken down by bacteria and other living organisms in the environment.

Brassicas: cabbages, Brussels sprouts, cauliflowers, kale, turnips, swedes, cress, salad, rape and mustards. All are closely related and are members of the 'Brassica' family of plants.

Compaction: where soil is packed down due to weight from above.

Crucifer: a member of the family *Cruciferae*. This includes the cabbage family, ornamentals such as wallflowers, and others.

Cucurbit: a member of the cucumber family – *Cucurbitaceae* – also including marrows, courgettes, squashes and melons.

Double digging: cultivating the soil to a depth of two spits (a spit is the depth of a spade).

Dripline/seep-hose: an underground or surface watering system.

Earthing up: heaping earth up around the base of a plant.

Green manure: a crop that is grown to incorporate into the soil.

Grub out: dig up and remove roots and stumps.

Gypsum: calcium sulphate, used to break up clay soils that do not need liming.

Harden off: gradually acclimatise indoor-grown plants to outdoor conditions before planting them out into the soil.

Herbicide: a chemical weedkiller.

Leaf mould: decomposed leaves.

Microclimate: the weather conditions of a small defined area.

Modules: seed/seedling tray divided up into compartments.

Mulch: any material spread over the soil.

Organic: a method of growing plants which avoids the use of chemical pesticides and artificial fertilisers.

Overwinter: survive the winter.

pH: a measure of the acidity of the soil. A pH of 7 is taken to be neutral; a soil with a pH of less than 7 is said to be acid, while a pH figure of more than 7 is said to be alkaline.

Photosynthesis: the process by which a green plant is able to make carbohydrates from water and carbon dioxide, using light as an energy source and chlorophyll to absorb the light.

Plant nutrient: any of the mineral substances that are absorbed by the roots of plants for nourishment.

Resting bodies: thick-walled structures containing fungal spores. Such 'bodies' are able to withstand drought, cold and other unfavourable conditions.

Rhizomorphs: conspicuous hard black strands, made up of fungal hyphae and looking like a plant root. These grow through the soil to spread the fungus from plant to plant.

Rootstock: a plant which provides the roots for another variety of the same plant, which is grafted on to it.

Scorzonera: a root vegetable with black slender roots.

Seed drill: a narrow, shallow depression made in the soil, by the edge of a rake or other tool, for sowing seed into.

Shelter-belt: trees or shrubs grown to protect other plants from the wind.

Silica crystals: hydrated silica used for absorbing moisture.

Soil pan: a hard layer below the soil surface, often only 30 cm to 45 cm below the surface.

Stock plant: a plant grown to provide cuttings for propagation.

Tares: a kind of vetch, in the pea family. Grown in gardens as a green manure.

Tilth: a fine, crumbly surface layer of soil.

Tines: the points or prongs of a fork or harrow.

Water table: the level in the soil below which the soil is saturated by ground water.

Index   Chapter headings are in bold type